Daniel

Daniel

The Son of God, The Son of Man

Copyright © Paul Blackham

The right of Paul Blackham to be identified as author of this work has been asserted by him in accordance with the Copyright, Designs and Patents Act 1988

First published 2009

All Rights Reserved. No part of this publication may be reproduced or transmitted in any form or by any means, electronic or mechanical including photocopying, recording, or any information storage and retrieval system, without permission in writing from the publisher.

Unless otherwise stated biblical quotations are taken from the Holy Bible, New International Version, Copyright © 1973, 1978, 1984 International Bible Society, used by permission of Zondervan Bible Publishers.

Scripture quotations marked (NLT) are taken from the Holy Bible, New Living Translation, Copyright © 1966. Used by permission of Tyndale House Publishers, Inc., Wheaton, Illinois 60189. All rights Reserved.

ISBN No: 978-1-905975-22-8

Published by Biblical Frameworks

Reg. Office: 23 Coe Lane, Tarleton, Preston, PR4 6HH.

Cover design, typesetting and production management by Verité CM Ltd, Worthing, West Sussex UK +44 (0) 1903 241975

Illustrations by Richard Thomas

Printed in England

Biblical Frameworks is registered in England No: 5712581
Charity No: 1116805.

Daniel

Contents

Introductory thoughts from Paul Blackham 5

All about Book by Book 7

An introduction to Daniel 9

Study 1 Praise be to the Name of God forever Daniel 1-2 15

Study 2 "The fourth looks like a Son of God" Daniel 3-4 31

Study 3 "My God sent His Angel" Daniel 5-6 43

Study 4 "One like the Son of Man" Daniel 7-8 59

Study 5 "A Man dressed in linen" Daniel 9-10 75

Study 6 "The Great Prince who protects your people" Daniel 10:10-12:13 89

Suggested Answers to the Bible Study questions...107

Daniel in the Lions Den

Daniel

I. Introductory thoughts from Paul Blackham

The longest chapter in the Bible is all about... the Bible! Psalm 119 is all about the wonder of the Word of God. Verse 103 shows us the heart of someone who really loved the Bible. He cries out to the LORD God:

Psalm 119:103 - "How sweet are your words to my taste, sweeter than honey to my mouth!"

Whether you are reading the Bible alone or in some kind of group with others, expect to be thrilled by the words of the Living God. This is not like reading any other book. When we read and study the Bible the ultimate Author can be present with you, showing you His words and applying them to you.

Thousands of small groups are starting up all over the world – but what is it that is going to sustain them? It has to be the Bible.

So often, people don't quite know what to do with these small groups. Meeting together, sharing testimonies and experiences or sharing the odd verse is ultimately too sparse a diet to sustain people's spiritual needs in the long run, and really help them to grow.

What is needed is confidence in the Bible, and the ability to go to a *book* of the Bible rather than just an isolated verse. Each book of the Bible was written with a purpose, and it is only as we digest it as a book that we understand the real message, purpose, direction, storyline and characters.

It's a lot easier than people often think. You might think, "Oh, I can't manage a whole book of the Bible", but what we're trying to do in Book by Book is to break it down and show that it's easy.

The Bible was written not for specialists, not for academics – it was written for the regular believers, down the ages.

The world is in desperate need for answers. How can the world live at peace? How can we live together with justice and truth and compassion? There are so many religions and so much division and bloodshed: what is the real and living way that takes us to the Living God who can give us all a new beginning?

The Bible is the answer of the Living God to all our questions.

Our desire is that many Christians would experience the joy and confidence in the Scriptures that is found throughout Psalm 119 - "How sweet are your words to my taste, sweeter than honey to my mouth!"

II. All about Book by Book

a. What is Book by Book?

Book by Book is a Bible Study resource with accompanying DVD. It has been designed principally for use in small groups, but can also be used for personal study or larger group situations.

b. The structure of Book by Book

The Study Guide

The Study Guide provides the following features for each section of study:

- A Key Truth to focus on the most important truth in that section of the Bible Book.
- A Mind-Map diagram giving an overview of the study.
- An explanation of the Bible text, divided under suitable headings.
- Further Questions, to stimulate deeper thought and discussion.
- A week of suggested daily Bible readings to fill out and explore the themes from the study.
- A Bible Study, with detailed questions, designed to lead the individual or group deeper into the text.
- A Bible Study answers section at the back of the study guide, for extra help if need be.

The DVD

Key features provided on each DVD are as follows:

- There is a 15 minute discussion on the DVD linked to each section of the Study Guide Bible passage
- The on-screen host is Richard Bewes, with co-host Paul Blackham. A specially invited guest joins them in the Bible discussions.

Daniel

C. Some tips on how to use Book by Book

The beauty of Book by Book is that it offers not only great Biblical depth, but also flexibility of approach to study. Whether you are preparing to lead a small group, or study alone you will find many options open to you.

And it doesn't matter if you are a new Christian or more experienced at leading Bible studies, Book by Book can be adapted to your situation. You don't need to be a specially trained leader.

Group study: preparing

- Select your study (preferably in the order of the book!)
- Watch the DVD programmes
- Read the commentary
- Use the suggested Bible questions…

…or formulate your own questions (the mind maps and key truths are a great guide for question structure)

Group study: suggested session structure

We recommend you set aside about an hour for each study

- 5 minutes – read the relevant section of the Bible
- 15 minutes – Watch the DVD programme
- 30 minutes – work through the Bible study questions (either your own or the ones in the guide), allowing time for discussion
- 10 minutes – If the study got the group thinking about wider issues of life today, Then consider the Further Questions to stimulate a broader discussion
- Taking it further – Suggest that group members look at some of the Daily Readings to follow up on the theme of the study

Given the volume of material you may even choose to take two weeks per study – using the DVD to generate discussion for one week and the Bible Study questions for the next.

Individual study

There is no set way to conduct personal study – here are some ideas:

- Select your study (preferably in the order of the book!)
- Read the Bible passage and related commentary.
- Try looking at the Mind-Map diagrams and seeing how the book has a structure.
- Take a look at the Key Truths and decide if they are the same conclusions you had reached when you read the book.
- Perhaps focus on the week of daily Bible reading to help you to explore the rest of the Bible's teaching on the themes of each section of study.
- Work through the Bible Questions. Don't worry if you get stuck, there is an 'answers' section at the back of the guide!

Daniel

III. An introduction to Daniel

Imagine what it would be like to be abducted as a teenager, taken away from family and friends.

Imagine being kidnapped into slavery, stripped of your language and culture, brainwashed into a system that rejects everything that you love.

Imagine being used by people who have no concern for your life, who will constantly threaten you with execution.

Is it possible to go through all that and still be full of hope and life and integrity?

How could anyone endure such trauma while maintaining their own identity and character?

Thousands of the ancient saints went through the terrible trauma of exile when the armies of Babylon destroyed the temple of the Living God before their very eyes. Everything that had seemed certain and unmoving had fallen down.

How could the LORD God allow this to happen?

As the thousands were marched away from their little world to the centre of an alien empire, the 'camera lens' of the Bible zooms down onto one young man called Daniel. He was probably about 15 years of age and had clearly been zealous for the law of the LORD. What was all this like for him? What was his destiny in this turmoil?

Daniel shows us how to hold onto the reality of the LORD Jesus Christ in a world that we don't control, a world that is full of values and assumptions that are hostile to the ways of the Living God. He shows us how we keep our true identity as citizens of the everlasting Kingdom of Heaven when we are also citizens of earthly kingdoms that come and go. Daniel shows us how to work with integrity and excellence even when surrounded by colleagues who openly reject the Living God, colleagues who even plot to destroy us.

World history is filled with the rise and fall of kingdoms, multi-national companies, ideologies and empires. There are wars and rumours of wars,

earthquakes and famines. How can the church of the Living God stand firm in the middle of this turmoil? How can we hold onto the solid Rock in the chaotic sea of human history?

The great message of the Book of Daniel is that Jesus, the Son of Man, the King of the everlasting Kingdom, is on the throne of the universe – high above all the spiritual forces in the heavenly realms and high above all the earthly kings and kingdoms. The Son of Man has been given all authority and power from the Ancient of Days and is able to raise up or humble anybody He chooses – Daniel 7:13-14.

Year BC	Event	Reference	Daniel's age?
620	The birth of Daniel		
605	Daniel abducted into exile	Daniel 1	15
604 562	Nebuchadnezzar's dream Death of Nebuchadnezzar	Daniel 2	16 58
After Nebuchadnezzar it seems that Nabonidus ruled Babylon (555?-539) and appointed his son Belshazzar to be in charge of in his absence. In Persia, Cyrus came to power in 559 BC and ruled until 530 BC.			
549?	Daniel's dream of four beasts	Daniel 7	71
547?	Daniel's dream of the Ram and the Goat	Daniel 8	73
539	Belshazzar's feast	Daniel 5	81
It seems that Darius was made ruler of the Babylonian kingdom under the overall rule of Cyrus, ruler of the whole Persian Empire – see Daniel 9:1 & 10:1			
539/8	Daniel's Prayer and the 70 weeks vision.	Daniel 9	81
538/7?	The lion's den	Daniel 6	82
536/5	Daniel's vision of a Man with the vision of world history	Daniel 10 - 12	84
Here we assume that Daniel 10:1 refers to the third year after Cyrus took control of the Babylonian kingdom through Darius.			

Daniel has four great visions in the second half of this book, each unfolding the course and meaning of human history.

Daniel

		Main Theme of Vision	Historical Date	When in Daniel's life
1	Daniel 7	The Four Beasts	Belshazzar Year 1	Between Daniel 4 & 5
2	Daniel 8	A Ram and A Goat	Belshazzar Year 3	Between Daniel 4 & 5
3	Daniel 9	Seventy Sevens	Darius Year 1	Daniel 6
4	Daniel 10-12	All of Human History	Cyrus Year 3	Possibly after his retirement

The book of Daniel is filled with symbolism, whether in terms of animals, numbers or locations. So many of the visions and events can seem quite confusing until we remember the symbolic meaning of the numbers referred to. Below we have provided a brief outline of the Biblical meanings of some of the numbers we find in the book of Daniel.

4	If three is the number of the Trinity throughout the Bible, then we can see that when another is added we get four! Creation was the glorious moment when another was added to the Eternal Three – and so throughout the Bible the number four stands for the whole creation. There are four points to the compass: north, south, east and west (Luke 13:29). In Genesis 2:10-11 the river that watered the whole earth split into four great rivers. There are four winds throughout the earth (Jeremiah 49:36; Ezekiel 37:9; Daniel 7:2, 8:8, 11:4; Zechariah 2:6; Matthew 24:31; Mark 13:27; Revelation 7:1). There are four seasons throughout the year (Genesis 8:22; Deuteronomy 11:14). There are four heavenly living creatures (ruling cherubim) who keep watch over the whole earth and give the decisions of the Divine Son of Man (Ezekiel 1:5; Revelation 4:6-8, 5:6-8, 5:14, 6:1, 6:6, 7:11, 14:3, 15:7, 19:4). These four living creatures each have four faces (Ezekiel 1:6, 10, 15; 10:14). The tabernacle represented the whole creation and it was made of four materials (gold, silver, brass and wood).
6	Humanity was created on the sixth day (Genesis 1:26-31). Humanity works for six days (Exodus 20:9). The number of the beast is the number of humanity repeated three times – 666 (Revelation 13:16-18). There are 6 *miktam* psalms, each dealing with the fact that humanity must die, yet in Jesus the Messiah there is resurrection – Psalms 16, 56, 57, 58, 59, 60. The *miktam* psalms reach their powerful conclusion Psalm 60:11-12 - "Give us aid against the enemy, for the help of man is worthless. With God we shall gain the victory, and He will trample down our enemies."

7	The Biblical symbolism of the number seven is 'perfection'. Seven (Hebrew Sheva or Sheba) comes from a root (S-B-A) meaning full or complete or satisfied – see Leviticus 26:18. Thus the whole work of creation is not complete until there has been the seventh day of rest. On that seventh day the LORD God is satisfied. There are seven seals perfectly holding the scroll of history in the Book of Revelation.
8	Eight is the number of new creation throughout the Bible. Jesus Himself rose from the dead on the eighth day, the first day of the new week. The final festival of the Levitical feasts, the feast of tents when they would have looked forward to the city with foundations[1], was an eight day feast. Circumcision, which was a sign of new birth and new creation (see Colossians 2:9-12) occurred on the eighth day.
10	In the Bible the number 10 tends to be associated with totality and entirety. The Ten Commandments stand in for the entirety of the whole Law of Moses. In Revelation 2:10, to suffer for ten days means that you will face complete suffering, ending in death.
12	The number 12 is associated with kingdoms and government, which is why there are 12 tribes of Israel, 12 apostles and 12 foundations in the city of God. This is also why time is divided up around the number 12. Even those cultures that rebel against the Living God still want to feel that time and history is ordered and governed. We generally prefer a clock face with the 12 numbers visible to us, rather than a digital readout so that we are aware of the government of time. Even the way the year is organized into 12 months and 12 signs of the zodiac – all these patterns point to the deep symbolic structures in the universe.
$3^{1}/_{2}$ [2]	If the perfect unit of time is a week (and we see time divided up into 'sevens' in the book of Daniel), then a half unit of time has two meanings: first, it is far less than perfect: it is a bad time, a time of suffering and persecution; second, it is not very long: it is 'only' half a 'seven', half a 'week' of time. Elijah was on the run from a godless state for three and a half years – 1 Kings 17-18. The terrible times of persecution predicted in Daniel last for 'a time, times and half a time'. We get this same time measurement in Daniel 12:7 and Revelation 12:14 (and see also Revelation 11:9-11). It can appear as 42 months, as in Revelation 11:2 or even as 1260 days, as in Revelation 11:3 and 12:6.[3]

---

1 See Hebrews 11:8-16
2 Sometimes stated as "a time, times and half a time" or as 42 months.
3 We might note that In Daniel 9:27 the troubled times occur "in the middle of the seven", which also indicates a period of three and a half.

The Studies

The insanity of autonomy

Daniel

Study 1 Praise be to the Name of God forever

Daniel 1-2

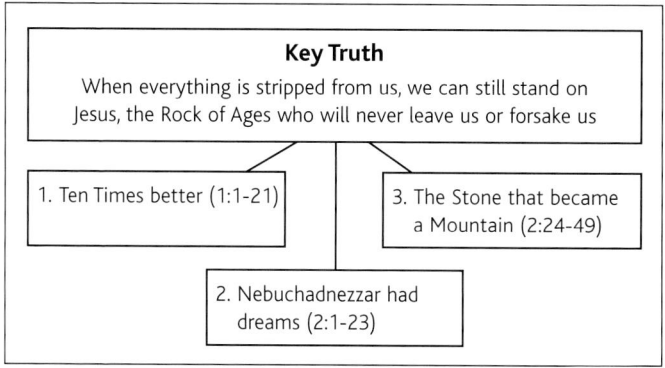

1. Ten Times better (Chapter 1:1-21)

The book of Daniel begins with a massive catastrophe, an event that would shake the faith and even sanity of the saints. Consider how the church of the Living God had triumphed over her adversaries in so many battles in the past. Remember how she was delivered out of Egypt and how the Angel of the LORD humiliated the mighty superpower of Egypt at the Red Sea. Remember what happened in Isaiah chapters 36-39 when the Angel of the LORD single-handedly destroyed a huge Babylonian army when Jerusalem was threatened.

The book of Daniel begins with the very opposite condition: the LORD sides with the king of Babylon over against Jerusalem and the church! It seems impossible and unthinkable. We cannot begin to imagine what this must have felt like for Daniel and his companions.

The sheer spiritual trauma of this Exile was very hard to bear. It had been threatened and predicted for hundreds of years… but it had finally happened. Think of the prediction made by the LORD in the book of Leviticus, spoken more than 700 years before this time of Exile actually happened – Leviticus 26:31-34.

The ancient church was suffering severe judgement from the Living God. It would have been so hard to have lived through this. The unfaithfulness and unbelief of the ancient church had provoked the fierce anger of their Glorious LORD.

Nevertheless, we must remember that it was the LORD who did this. However bad this experience may have been, yet it was all still under the control of the Living God. Their heavenly Father was chastising His people, but He was still their Father and He was still ruling over history and all the kingdoms of the earth.

In verses 3-4, we learn that Nebuchadnezzar ordered that the very finest young people should be taken captive and trained to be part of the imperial staff in Babylon. Not only did they have to leave their land, but also their language, their culture, their family, their friends, their temple. They were abducted to be used by others. Every marker of their own identity seemed to be taken away.

What can hold you together when everything that has formed you, everything that supports you, is taken away?

Few of us have to deal with such a profound dismantling of the scaffolding of our souls, yet that is what Daniel and his friends had to face. Even their very names were taken from them.

Think of their Hebrew names for a moment: Daniel, Hananiah, Mishael and Azariah.

Hebrew Name	Meaning	Babylonian Name	Meaning
Daniel	God my judge	Belteshazzar	blessed by the god Bel[4]
Hananiah	Grace from the LORD	Shadrach	Aku's[5] command
Mishael	He who is asked for	Meshach	Guest of the king[6]
Azariah	He hears the LORD	Abednego	Servant of Nego[7]

---

4 His name is very like the name of the later king of Babylon, Belshazzar, who we meet in chapter 5 – whose name means 'blessed by Bel', a Babylonian god – see Jeremiah 51:44.
5 Aku was a Babylonian god
6 Mishael did not want to be a "guest" of Nebuchadnezzar
7 Nego or Nebo was a Babylonian god

Daniel

Each of their Hebrew names had such a precious character, reminding them of their special relationship with the LORD God. Their Babylonian names were a mockery of their life in the ancient church. Daniel looked to God as his judge, but now he was supposed to look to the god Bel for blessing! Hananiah received grace from the LORD, but now was a command of a pagan god. Mishael was somebody whose company was asked for, but now he was the forced guest at the behest of a foreign tyrant. Azariah would hear the Voice of the LORD, but was now the servant of a false god.

How could these ancient saints reject these 'new' names? They were about to be drowned in a pagan culture… was it possible to remember that Jesus is LORD of the whole earth?

Verse 8 – "But Daniel resolved not to defile himself with the royal food and wine".

Not only was food very important in the ancient Law of Moses, but the people we have fellowship with around a table define who we are. Table fellowship is taken very seriously throughout the Bible. In 1 Kings 18:19 the prophets of Baal are described as those who "eat at Jezebel's table" – meaning that the prophets acknowledged her as their leader and host. In this way, Daniel would have been nervous of simply becoming someone who 'ate at Nebuchadnezzar's table' rather than someone who enjoyed daily fellowship with the LORD Jesus.

Daniel found an area of life that would keep him connected to the church of the Living God. The book of Leviticus had specific rules regarding the foods that were clean and unclean under the covenant of Sinai – see Leviticus chapters 11 & 17. Daniel wasn't able to live by all the laws of the LORD, but at least this was one area that he could try to keep for the LORD Jesus.

It might have seemed impossible to ask for this, but (verse 9) the Living God over-ruled the heart of the official, and permission was granted.

In verses 10-16 we see that they were given a probationary period.[8]

---

8   Notice that the time of testing was for 10 days. In the Bible the number 10 tends to be associated with totality and entirety. It is as if Daniel and his friends were given the most careful and total examination. The verdict that they were ten times better is also to be noted.

Whether through the special blessing of the LORD or the superiority of a water/vegetarian diet, these saints looked far healthier than all the others.[9]

With great courage and trust, these four young men made a stand for the Way of the LORD... and He blessed them in their situation (verse 17).

To these four young men God gave knowledge and understanding of all kinds of literature and learning. And Daniel could understand visions and dreams of all kinds.

The Bible teaches us that all our gifts and abilities come from the Living God – not just the 'spiritual' ones that we might use on a Sunday! See Isaiah 28:23-29; Deuteronomy 8:17-18 and Exodus 35:30-35. In the situation that the LORD God placed them, He gave them the ability to do well. In the case of Daniel, he was also given a highly unusual ability: to understand visions and dreams. Later we will see the vital significance of this rare gift.

When their time of training was completed, they were presented to king Nebuchadnezzar and they were found to be the very best students of all (verses 18-21). We know that our generous Father grants wisdom to His children whenever they ask (James 1:5), and these four young men had ten times more wisdom than those who trusted in their own wisdom or the wisdom of the pagan gods (verse 20).

Daniel remained serving in that royal palace for more than 60 years until he was employed by the Persian empire instead by Darius under King Cyrus (see verse 21).

2. Nebuchadnezzar had dreams (Chapter 2:1-23)

Chapter 2 opens with the kind of experience that so many of us have been through: a troubled night. Nebuchadnezzar had a very vivid dream,

---

9   This is surely a challenge to those of us who are used to eat 'luxurious' or 'junk' food all the time. For many of us, our diets come at great expense (not so much for our own finances but for those who produce this food and for the environment). Used to eating quantities of meat for nearly every meal, our diets place a huge demand not only the world but also on our own bodies. What if, in the Name of Jesus, we were to simplify and reduce our basic diet? What if simple vegetables, bread, pasta, rice and fruit were to form the majority of our food? What if water (with no additions) were to be our standard drink? See, e.g. the information on www.peopleandplanet.net. The World Wildlife Fund has a fascinating Living Planet report looking at some of the issues of consumerism. Christian Aid has valuable resources www.christianaid.org.uk.

Daniel

after which he was unable to get back to sleep. Therefore, he decided that his top experts should not sleep either and "the magicians, enchanters, sorcerers and astrologers" were all roused out of bed as well.

The difficulty was that Nebuchadnezzar demanded not only to know the meaning of his dream… but they first had to tell him what he had dreamed! (verses 3-9). Furthermore, if they were unable to do this, then they would be killed in a very thorough way.

It is worth noting the different realms of expertise that Nebuchadnezzar was calling upon.

Magicians

Before the book of Daniel, these 'magicians' are exclusively **Egyptian** magic specialists.[10] They seemed to be capable of works of genuine magical power and clearly Pharaoh expected them to have expertise in the area of dreams.

- Genesis 41:8 "In the morning his mind was troubled, so he sent for all the *magicians* and wise men of Egypt. Pharaoh told them his dreams, but no one could interpret them for him."
- Exodus 8:7, 18 – "But the *magicians* did the same things by their secret arts; they also made frogs come up on the land of Egypt… But when the *magicians* tried to produce gnats by their secret arts, they could not. And the gnats were on men and animals."

Enchanters

It is difficult to know the exact nature of these occult experts, because they are mentioned only here in the book of Daniel – 2:10; 2:27; 4:7; 5:7, 11, 15. This category may come from a Hebrew word meaning to lisp, so some kind of speaking or muttering seems to have been involved in this magic.

Sorcerers

This is also a category of occult specialist that was present in the courts of Egypt (Exodus 7:11). This kind of practice attracted the most severe

---

10 They are also mentioned in Daniel 1:20

condemnation from the Living God (Exodus 22:18; Deuteronomy 18:10), most likely because of the vile and unjust activities that their work involved.

- 2 Chronicles 33:6 "(Manasseh) sacrificed his sons in the fire in the Valley of Ben Hinnom, practiced *sorcery*, divination and witchcraft, and consulted mediums and spiritists. He did much evil in the eyes of the Lord, provoking him to anger."
- Malachi 3:5 "So I will come near to you for judgment. I will be quick to testify against *sorcerers*, adulterers and perjurers, against those who defraud laborers of their wages, who oppress the widows and the fatherless, and deprive aliens of justice, but do not fear me," says the Lord Almighty."

Astrologers (Chaldeans/Babylonians)

This forth category of 'wise man' is the most difficult to pin down because the Hebrew word is simply the word used to refer to men from Chaldea/Babylon. It may well be that, due to the antiquity of the Babylonian civilization, the title of 'Chaldean' contained the idea of great wisdom or being an 'elder'.

Nebuchadnezzar had collected the very best and wisest experts from all around the world with a variety of specialisations. Today the French are often associated with cooking, and in a similar way it seems that in these areas of special power and knowledge the Egyptians were seen to have great expertise. Whether the practitioners were really Egyptian or not, the title of 'magician' was associated with the Egyptians. Nebuchadnezzar had Egyptian magicians, Babylonian elders together with the mysterious enchanters and the cruelly experimental sorcerers: whatever area of research and wisdom, this leader of a world superpower wanted to ensure he had the best available.

The ability to genuinely understand and interpret dreams was a very highly prized ability in the ancient world, and even today there are many books and psychological theories about dreams. Modern experts tend to take a very narrow view of dreams, seeing them as a kind of 'message' sent from within us about the kind of tensions and concerns that we might have. In a very individualistic age we should not be surprised at such a narcissistic view of dreams, but for most of the world down through history dreams have been seen in a much bigger context.[11] Covering everything from the individual troubles of the dreamer ranging right up to prophecies given from the heavenly realms, dreams were seen in a larger, cosmic framework.

Although it is often said that "an uninterpreted dream is like an unread letter"[12], the Bible does not regard all dreams as reliable sources of wisdom. In fact the Bible warns us not to trust all our dreams. Sometimes our dreams are nothing but reflections of our own desires or needs (Isaiah 29:8). Ecclesiastes 5:3 seems to say that our dreams can be generated by having too many cares and pressures – and that these dreams are equivalent to the many words of a fool. Psalm 73:20 equates our dreams with mere fleeting fantasies (see also Job 20:8). The LORD through Jeremiah is very direct in exposing the delusions that we invent in our dreams (Jeremiah 23:25-29). In Daniel 2:45, Daniel reports that Nebuchadnezzar's dream was true, implying that not all dreams are truthful. This is important because there are those who diligently record all their dreams in the belief that all of them contain important, truthful wisdom. Some dreams come from 'idols' that mislead us with false insights (Zechariah 10:2).[13]

So, rather than simply believing, recording and analysing all our dreams, as if they were an infallible source of wisdom and revelation, we need to look to the written Words of the Living God to provide the rock of clarity and truth. From this Rock of stability, we will be able to see what is true and false, what is from the Living God and what are simply the delusions/desires of our own minds (or even dreams from idols).

With all those warnings in mind, the Bible gives many, many examples of the Living God delivering important warnings, guidance and prophecy

---

11 Dream 'dictionaries' were used in both India and China before 1000BC. Many rules were given about the nature of the dreams and how to tell a 'true' from a 'false' dream. For example, if several dreams were dreamed in a single night, only the last was to be unravelled. A dream from early in the night pertained to far distant events (beyond a year), whereas dreams at the end of the sleep cycle involved things that were already taking place. In some world traditions dreams were thought to be sent not only from 'the gods' but also from long dead or yet-to-be family members!

12 Rabbi Hisda from *The Babylonian Talmud*, written between 200BC and 200AD.

13 Idols here might cover not only the false gods and demons of the heavenly realms, but also the idols of money, status, popularity and beauty that bewitch so many of us.

through dreams.[14] It seems to be that when a person has such a dream, they realize that their dream has a weight and urgency beyond the normal delusions of the mind. Nebuchadnezzar couldn't sleep after his God-given dream (Daniel 2:1) and Pilate's wife was greatly troubled through her dream about Jesus (Matthew 27:19). Joseph taught that the LORD will repeat the dream in a different way if the matter has been firmly decided by God – Genesis 41:32. To some (especially 'unbelievers') the Lord's dreams seem to be complex and need the interpretation of a gifted saint, but to others they can seem very simple and direct[15].

> Matthew 2:12-13 – "And having been warned in a *dream* not to go back to Herod, (The Magi) returned to their country by another route. When they had gone, an angel of the Lord appeared to Joseph in a *dream*. "Get up," he said, "take the child and his mother and escape to Egypt. Stay there until I tell you, for Herod is going to search for the child to kill him.""

How is a vision different to a dream? A vision seems to come upon its recipient when they are fully awake and the visions do not seem to have the level of obscurity often found in the dreams.[16] However, visions also require careful discernment, for they also may be wicked or false – Jeremiah 14:14; 23:16; Lamentations 2:14; Ezekiel 12:24; 13:1-23; 21:29; 22:28.

---

14 Jacob's dream of the stairway to heaven – Genesis 28:10-22; Jacob's dream of the goats – Genesis 31:10-13; Joseph's Messianic dreams – Genesis 37:5-9; The dreams of the cupbearer and baker – Genesis 40:1-23; Pharaoh's dreams of the future famine – Genesis 41:1-8; possibly the dream overheard by Gideon in Judges 7:13-16; Solomon's dream of the LORD Jesus – 1 Kings 3:5-15; Daniel's dreams from Daniel 7:1; Joseph, the husband of Mary, had more recorded dreams than anybody else in the whole Bible – Matthew 1:20; 2:13; 2:19; 2:22; The Magi who came to worship Jesus – Matthew 2:12.

15 Matthew 1:20 "After Joseph considered this, an angel from the Lord appeared to him in a dream and said, 'Joseph son of David, do not be afraid to take Mary home as your wife, because what is conceived in her is of the Holy Spirit'". See also Genesis 20:3-6; Genesis 31:24.

16 See Abraham in Genesis 15:1-3; Jacob in Genesis 46:2-4; Balaam in Numbers 24:1-9; Samuel in 1 Samuel 3:1-18; the whole of Isaiah's prophecy is described as a vision – 2 Chronicles 32:32 & Isaiah 1:1; Ezekiel has many visions – 1:1ff; note 8:4; 11:22-25; 43:1-5; Daniel in Daniel 2:19; in Daniel 7 he has a strange mixture of dreams and visions; Daniel 8:1ff; 10:1ff. The prophets often received the Word of the LORD through visions Obadiah 1:1; Micah 1:1; Nahum 1:1; Zechariah 1:8… and then another Zechariah in Luke 1:22. The LORD continued to speak in visions in the New Testament – Ananias in 9:12; Cornelius in 10:1-8; Peter in 10:9-20; Paul and the Macedonian in Acts 16:6-10; Paul again in Acts 18:9-11; Paul in 2 Corinthians 12:1; John in Revelation (note 9:17).

Daniel

In Numbers 12:6 the LORD says that He speaks to His prophets in visions as well as dreams[17].

Like Joseph in Genesis 40 & 41, Daniel was granted the wisdom of the Living God to unravel the dreams that the LORD had given.[18] It is very important to note what the astrologers say to the king's demand for them to both tell him his dream and interpret it:

> There is not a man on earth who can do what the king asks! No king, however great and mighty, has ever asked such a thing of any magician or enchanter or astrologer. *What the king asks is too difficult. No one can reveal it to the king except the gods, and they do not live among men.*

This is extremely important. No human being could possibly do what the king asks and even though the gods could do it, yet they do not live amongst human beings. The only solution to the problem then is for the Living God to appear among human beings. Is there really a Living God who could leave the unknown and inaccessible realms of heaven and speak with mere human creatures… a Son of Man who would live among men? The book of Daniel will answer that question with a glorious YES!

King Nebuchadnezzar doesn't like the astrologers' answer so he orders the execution of all the royal advisers, including Daniel and his friends (verses 12-15). However, Daniel knows the Living God who really does live among His people, so after prayer, Daniel received the answer in a night vision. Daniel's prayer of praise is a wonderful first answer to the challenge of the astrologers.

In the first portion of this prayer of praise Daniel acknowledges how exalted and glorious is the Living God of his fathers. The LORD God has total power over the seasons and human kingdoms. All the wisdom and knowledge that human beings have comes from Him and the very deepest and darkest things are known to Him. Yet, in the second part of

---

17 We also learn here why Moses did not have any dreams and visions.

18 If we consider the three great dream specialists in the Bible, some interesting parallels emerge – Joseph, Daniel and Mary's husband Joseph (Joseph A.D.). In the case of all three, other people seem to have dreams around them, almost as if, as one person said, they acted as 'lightning conductors' for dreams. In addition, and crucially, Magi surrounded all three: wise men from the nations. In the case of Joseph A.D., the Magi had genuine wisdom, able to not only interpret a dream for themselves but also read the stars and worship Jesus. Joseph A.D., obviously, was the greatest of the dream specialists in the Bible.

the prayer Daniel indicates that this Living God does 'live among men'! He has given His power and knowledge of the deepest secrets to Daniel.

As followers of Jesus, the Divine Son of Man, we know the Living God who has all power and understands the deepest truths. The truth beyond imagination is that as we follow and obey Jesus, the Eternal, Divine Holy Spirit will actually live within us and set up a home for the God the Father and God the Son (John 14:23). Yes, the One True God over all lives within those who follow the Way of Jesus! We can live His life and do His truth knowing that He has prepared all our steps in advance. Whatever knowledge and power we need, He will give us if we will obediently follow His Way.

3. The Stone that became a Mountain (Chapter 2:24-49)

By this stage of the story we are all sitting on the edge of our seats – could Daniel have really been given the secret of the dream? What was this dream? What could it possibly means?

Arioch (the commander of the king's guard, and Nebuchadnezzar are told the unlikely truth that Daniel is able to do the impossible. However, Daniel wants to make it clear who the glory needs to be directed to: "No wise man, enchanter, magician or diviner can explain to the king the mystery he has asked about, but *there is a God in heaven who reveals mysteries… The Revealer of Mysteries showed you what is going to happen*. As for me, this mystery has been revealed to me, not because I have greater wisdom than other living men, but so that you, O king, may know the interpretation" (Verses 27-30).

The first thing to realize is that the Living God gave this dream to Nebuchadnezzar in order to reveal mysteries to him. He wanted to show the king that in spite of what the astrologers and wise men had to say, there is a Living God who will deal with human beings and reveal His mysteries to them.

In his dream Nebuchadnezzar had seen a dazzling statue.

Its head was made of gold.
Its chest and arms were made of silver.
Its stomach and thighs were made of bronze.
Its legs were made of iron.
Its feet were made of iron and clay.

Daniel

Nebuchadnezzar is told that although his kingdom is represented by the head of gold, yet other kingdoms/empires are coming which will replace his own. We might be able to identify the kingdoms of verses 39-43 as follows[19]:

Gold head – Babylonian empire.
Silver chest – Persian empire.
Bronze stomach – Greek empire.[20]
Iron/clay legs and feet – Roman empire.

While these kingdoms rise and fall, while they overtake one another, there is another kingdom on the scene. The great statue of the human kingdoms towers over the landscape, but a rock is cut out of a mountain (2:45) that becomes the great mountain that destroys the human kingdoms. While the human empires focus on their own survival, this other kingdom was growing, almost unnoticed, right among them.

Although the four kingdoms mentioned here may well be the Babylonian, Persian, Greek and Roman empires, yet, at a deeper level, the unstable statue represents all the kingdoms of the world. Throughout the Bible the number four represents the whole world.[21] This statue is fundamentally about the kingdoms of the world, not only in that ancient age, but also in every age. The kingdoms of the world may seem to be full of glory and permanence, yet ultimately they have no lasting foundations. They all

---

19 Sometimes people disagree about these designations and suggest different historical patterns. This same pattern of disagreement comes up time after time through the book of Daniel. As we will see, the key is not identifying all the historical details in these symbolic visions, but rather understanding the big picture. The kingdoms of humanity come and go, but the Kingdom of Jesus lasts forever. At the end, the Kingdom of Jesus inherits the whole earth, leaving no room for any other kingdoms.

20 See Daniel 8:20-21

21 If three is the number of the Trinity throughout the Bible, then we can see that when another is added we get four! Creation was the glorious moment when another was added to the Eternal Three – and so throughout the Bible the number four stands for the whole creation. There are four points to the compass: north, south, east and west (Luke 13:29). In Genesis 2:10-11 the river that watered the whole earth split into four great rivers. There are four winds throughout the earth (Jeremiah 49:36; Ezekiel 37:9; Daniel 7:2, 8:8, 11:4; Zechariah 2:6; Matthew 24:31; Mark 13:27; Revelation 7:1). There are four seasons throughout the year (Genesis 8:22; Deuteronomy 11:14). There are four heavenly living creatures (ruling cherubim) who keep watch over the whole earth and give the decisions of the Divine Son of Man (Ezekiel 1:5; Revelation 4:6-8, 5:14, 6:1, 6:6, 7:11, 14:3, 15:7, 19:4). These four living creatures each have four faces (Ezekiel 1:6, 10, 15; 10:14). The tabernacle represented the whole creation and it was made of four materials (gold, silver, brass and wood).

have 'feet of clay'. In each age there may seem to be empires that will never pass away – the Roman empire; the British empire; the communist empire; the capitalist empire – yet, they all fall down. None of them are the kingdom made without human hands (2:34, 45).

The downfall of the kingdoms of the earth is not finally because of their own inherent weakness, but because there is another Kingdom that pushes them aside. In verse 37-38 Nebuchadnezzar is told that the earth and all that is in it has been placed under his hands. This reminds us of the original authority given to humanity when the universe was created back in Genesis 1:26-28. This power and authority belongs to the Son of Man, whose kingdom will never pass away. All the authority of the world belongs to Him and all the pretenders must finally give way to Him.

The kingdom of the Living God is cut from a mountain[22] without human hands. This is a kingdom built without the efforts of human beings. When the LORD God was describing how an altar might be built for Him, it had to be made with stones that were not worked by human hands – Exodus 20:25 – "If you make an altar of stones for me, do not build it with dressed stones, for you will defile it if you use a tool on it."[23] (see Deuteronomy 27:5; Joshua 8:31). He does not rely on human power and He is not served by human hands (Acts 17:25). When the temple was being built, there had to be no sound of human tools at work – (1 Kings 6:7) "In building the temple, only blocks dressed at the quarry were used, and no hammer, chisel or any other iron tool was heard at the temple site while it was being built."[24]

Although Daniel tells the king in verse 45 that this dream is about what will happen in the future, it is not just about events in the distant future. Throughout the book of Daniel we learn that the Kingdom of the Living

---

22 What is the mountain that the rock is cut from? (Isaiah 2:3; Micah 4:2)

23 Interestingly, when they came to make the golden calf in order to worship the devil, we are told (Exodus 32:4) "(Aaron) took what they handed him and made it into an idol cast in the shape of a calf, *fashioning it with a tool*. Then they said, "These are your gods, O Israel, who brought you up out of Egypt." This pagan worship was very definitely the work of human hands! See also Isaiah 37:19 & 44:12 on human hands and idol worship.

24 Note also how Paul refers us to this teaching in order to understand that our resurrection bodies are also produced without human hands – 2 Corinthians 5:1.

Daniel

God, the stone, was growing right among them. Over and over again in the book of Daniel we are told that the Divine King rules over all the human kingdoms, that the empires of history – even the heavenly powers of angels and principalities – all fall under the rule of the Kingdom of the Living God.

In the Bible, Babylon always seems to represent the world in rebellion against the LORD God. Yet, Daniel chapter 2 ends with the LORD's man made ruler over the entire province of Babylon (verse 48). Not even Babylon is beyond His control.

Indeed, the LORD's Man, Jesus, rules over the whole world, even over the godless empires and multinational companies, the warlords and the media moguls, the politicians and the drug dealers, the slave traders and the opinion formers. He is the Crucified and Risen King of the kingdom that will never be destroyed (2:44).

The power of prayer

Study 1 Bible Questions

Daniel 2:14-23

1. Verse 14-15 – How was Daniel able to remain so calm when faced with sudden execution?
2. Verse 16 – How could this foreign slave boy dare to negotiate with the great king Nebuchadnezzar? Can we think of examples like this in our own lives where we need great courage, wisdom and tact as we serve the Living God?
3. Verse 17 – What was Daniel's first course of action in this crisis?
4. Verse 18 – What was the second course of action? Shouldn't he have spent his time doing some 'dream research'?
5. Verse 19 – The prayer was amazingly answered that very night while they were praying together. Can we recall any occasions when this has happened to us? Can we think of other occasions in the Bible when this has happened?
6. Verses 19-20 – What was Daniel's immediate reaction to the answered prayer?
7. Verse 20 – What qualities of the LORD God does Daniel first praise?
8. Verse 21 – What does Daniel mean by the two parts of his prayer in this verse? Why doesn't the LORD God give wisdom to the foolish?
9. Verses 22-23 – Even the very deepest and darkest secrets are obvious to the King of heaven. What impact would this night have had on the life of Daniel?

Daniel

Study 1 Further Questions

1. There are millions of people, including Christians, who are abducted into the sex industry today. Is it possible for a Christian to survive as a servant if Jesus even under such conditions of abuse and evil?

2. What role does diet have in our Christian discipleship? If we are seriously overweight (or underweight), what does that say about our godliness?

3. Does the LORD God still speak through dreams? How can we know whether a dream is sent from Him or just produced by a late nigh snack?

Study 1 Daily Readings

Day 1	2 Kings 23:31-24:7
Day 2	2 Kings 24:8-20
Day 3	2 Kings 25:1-30
Day 4	Psalm 137:1-9
Day 5	Daniel 1:1-21
Day 6	Daniel 2:1-23
Day 7	Daniel 2:24-49

The daily Bible readings are an opportunity to not only read through all of the material in the book under study, but also to read parts of the Bible that relate to the themes and issues that we have been considering. We try to make sure that we receive light from the whole Bible as we think through the key issues each week.

Greek sheep versus Persian rams

Daniel

Study 2 "The fourth looks like a Son of God"

Daniel 3-4

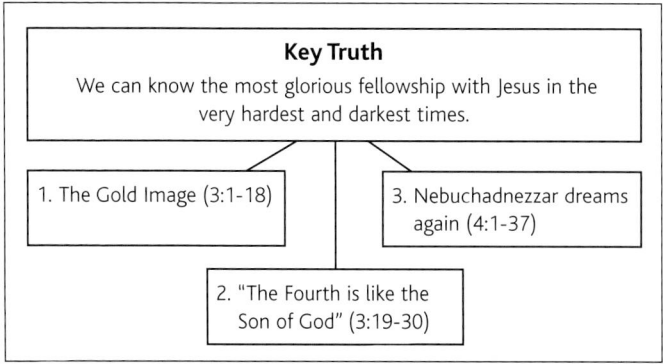

1. The Gold Image (Chapter 3:1-18)

The message of Nebuchadnezzar's dream had been very clear: all human kingdoms, no matter how glorious they appear to be, will pass away and they must all bow before the Kingdom of the Son of Man. Nebuchadnezzar had been told that his own kingdom, though 'golden', was to be replaced by other kingdoms.

Surely, Nebuchadnezzar would now act with much greater humility!

However, when we start to read chapter three of Daniel we are amazed at Nebuchadnezzar's actual response. It is as if he did not listen to Daniel's explanation of the dream and simply fixed on the bits he wanted to hear. All Nebuchadnezzar took from the dream was that he was the "king of kings", that the God of heaven had given him great power and that he was the "head of gold" (Daniel 2:37-38).

It is worth stopping for a moment to recognize how great Nebuchadnezzar really was. He is sometimes described as the greatest of all the leaders of Babylon/Iraq over its extremely long history. Even modern leaders of Iraq have looked back to Nebuchadnezzar as the highest standard of leadership. Nebuchadnezzar brought his empire into a golden age, building the world famous ancient wonder of the Hanging Gardens of Babylon. His architectural, cultural, military and economic achievements were remarkable. We can see why in his first dream he is acknowledged as the golden head, yet we can also see how his pride could run away with this idea.

Nebuchadnezzar still needed to learn to submit to the real King of kings whose kingdom is eternal. No matter how great he was in this passing age, yet he was a mere breath, withering grass, fleeting smoke.

Nebuchadnezzar thought that the problem with the statue in his dream was that it was made of mixed materials. If the whole image was made of gold, if the whole world was dominated by his empire in all ages, then he imagined it would be able to stand against the stone that becomes a mountain.

He had a golden image (of himself?) set up on the plain of Dura. The statue is dominated by the number 6: 60 cubits high and 6 cubits wide (90 feet by 9 feet, or 27 metres by 2.7 metres). The symbolism is clear. In the Bible six is the number of humanity, humanity falling short of the glory of the Living God.[25] Set on the flat plain, where it could be seen from far away, Nebuchadnezzar proclaims his human glory, demanding that all the different officials from all the provinces fall down and worship his image.

In verses 5, 7, 10 and 15 we are told of the wide range of musical instruments used in to summon everyone to worship Nebuchadnezzar's image – "the horn, flute, zither, lyre, harp, pipes and all kinds of music." However strange this list may sound to the modern reader we are to appreciate that this would have been an incredible audio experience, gathering together the best musical abilities from across a vast empire. It would have been overwhelming and deeply moving to be caught up into the awe inspiring multi-media presentation from Nebuchadnezzar.

---

25 Humanity was created on the sixth day (Genesis 1:26-31). Humanity works for six days (Exodus 20:9). The number of the beast is the number of humanity repeated three times – 666 (Revelation 13:16-18). There are 6 miktam psalms, each dealing with the fact that humanity must die, yet in Jesus the Messiah there is resurrection – psalms 16, 56, 57, 58, 59, 60. The miktam psalms reach their powerful conclusion Psalm 60:11-12 - "Give us aid against the enemy, for the help of man is worthless. With God we shall gain the victory, and He will trample down our enemies."

Daniel

Who could possible resist such a powerful display of the glory of the Babylonian empire?

Some of the Chaldeans (astrologers) noticed that the Jews were able to resist (3:8). The Jews knew of another King whose kingdom and glory and music was so inconceivably more awe inspiring than even the very greatest of all earthly glory and music. They could not worship what they knew was going to be pushed aside by the Kingdom of the Living God.

Shadrach, Meshach and Abednego, the friends of Daniel, were singled out for special condemnation (3:12) – "They neither serve your gods nor worship the image of gold you have set up."

Even when they are directly threatened with being burnt alive in a blazing furnace (verses 13-15), these saints refuse to share Jesus' glory with any creature (verses 16-18). Their words of reply are very interesting.

The Living God is always able to save His saints from any situation, yet for all kinds of reasons He does not always do that. This Living God has marked out for us the way of His Cross, and we take up our cross and follow Him. Some of us may be given the privilege of a martyr's death, whilst others may be permitted to enjoy His glorious presence in the fires of suffering. Whether we live or die, whether we are free or in prison, whether we may worship openly or secretly as follows of Jesus, yet we cannot acknowledge anyone or any object or any being or any idea as worthy of the glory that belongs to Jesus alone.

Remember that in the time it has taken you to read these pages, several followers of Jesus will have been murdered by forces and regimes that reject Jesus. Every hour brothers and sisters around the world will confess that even if they are not delivered from death yet even still they will not worship anyone or anything other than Jesus.

2. "The Fourth is like the Son of God" (Chapter 3:19-30)

Nebuchadnezzar does not take this reply very well! He is enraged and orders the blazing furnace to be made seven times hotter than normal.[26]

---

[26] Again, the Biblical symbolism of the number seven is 'perfection' or 'completion' - see Leviticus 26:18. In other words, Nebuchadnezzar wanted a 'perfectly hot' furnace! Seven (Hebrew Sheva or Sheba) comes from a root (S-B-A) meaning full or complete or satisfied. Thus the whole work of creation is not complete until there has been the seventh day of rest. On that seventh day the LORD God is satisfied. There are seven seals perfectly holding the scroll of history in the Book of Revelation.

The very best soldiers are summoned to throw these ancient Christians into the furnace, and the furnace is so hot that these strongest soldiers are killed by the heat (3:22).

It is interesting to note that Shadrach, Meshach and Abednego are wearing their Babylonian clothing – including trousers and turbans (verse 21).[27]

Nebuchadnezzar had positioned himself so that he would be able to watch these three saints as the fire consumed them… yet he was astonished to see a fourth figure with them:

> He answered and said, Lo, I see four men loose, walking in the midst of the fire, and they have no hurt; and the form of the fourth is *like the Son of God*.[28]

Sometimes people struggle to understand how Jesus could have been present and active in the Old Testament (before He was even born from Mary), yet of all the many times that we find Him in the Old Testament, perhaps more people recognize Him here than anywhere else! Matthew Henry explains this so well in his commentary on this verse.

> He appeared often in our nature before he assumed it in his incarnation, and never more seasonable, nor to give a more proper indication and presage of his great errand into the world in the fulness of time, than now, when, to deliver his chosen out of the fire, he came and walked with them in the fire. Note, Those that suffer for Christ have his gracious presence with them in their sufferings, even in the fiery furnace, even in the valley of the shadow of death, and therefore even there they need fear no evil. Hereby Christ showed that what is done against his people he takes as done against himself; whoever throws them into the furnace does, in effect, throw him in. I am Jesus, whom you are persecuting Isa. 63:9 [29].

One of the very deepest lessons in all of life comes home to us in this wonderful incident: we so often experience the very deepest and closest

---

27 Ezekiel 23:15.

28 The King James version of the Bible.

29 "In all their distress He too was distressed, and *the Angel of His Presence* saved them. In His love and mercy He redeemed them; He lifted them up and carried them all the days of old."

Daniel

fellowship with Jesus, the Crucified God, in the depths of suffering. When we walk through the valley of the shadow of death it is then that we feel Him with us more than before. To those living in darkness, the Light has shined. In the hottest furnace, when all hope is gone, the One who cried out in His dying darkness, will walk with us.

There are those who imagine that comfort, health and wealth are the signs of Jesus' presence and power, but those that have met the Living God in the shadow of the Cross, know that in the weakness, in the pain, in the persecution, in the sickness, in the loneliness He makes His power known.

Perhaps the most incredible part of this account is the fact that the three friends are in no rush to leave the furnace. In fact, Nebuchadnezzar has to command them to leave the furnace!

> Daniel 3:26 – Nebuchadnezzar then approached the opening of the blazing furnace and shouted, "Shadrach, Meshach and Abednego, servants of the Most High God, come out! Come here!"

So often we would not exchange our times of suffering for times of ease because of the fellowship we enjoy with Jesus in the hard times. This has been one of the common features of Christian testimony down through the ages. It is the message that Paul writes to the Corinthians in his second letter, especially in chapters 11 and 12.

> I will boast all the more gladly about my weaknesses, so that Christ's power may rest on me. That is why, for Christ's sake, I delight in weaknesses, in insults, in hardships, in persecutions, in difficulties. For when I am weak, then I am strong. (2 Corinthians 11:9-10)

When they came out of the furnace Nebuchadnezzar was amazed. They had been in the depths of the furnace but the fire had not harmed them in any way. Even the smell of the furnace was not left on their clothes. Jesus Himself promised in Luke 21:18 that although we may suffer all kinds of trials, yet no final harm will come to us. As we look into our future all we can see is the glorious light of a renewed creation in the presence of the Father and Jesus filled with the Spirit, living the life of the Kingdom forever and ever.

Even Nebuchadnezzar ends by acknowledging that Jesus, the Divine Angel of the Living God, is the Saviour of His servants, and that to trust in Him is right even if it means defying any civil or religious authority.

3. Nebuchadnezzar dreams again (4:1-37)

Chapter 4 begins in such an extraordinary way.

> King Nebuchadnezzar,
> To the peoples, nations and men of every language, who live in all the world: May you prosper greatly!

The chapter is literally a letter from Nebuchadnezzar to everybody in the whole world. He wanted to tell every human being that the kingdom of the Most High God is the only kingdom that lasts forever.

What brought this mighty and arrogant king to such a humble acknowledgement of the kingdom ruled over by the eternal Son of Man?

It all began with Nebuchadnezzar having another dream. Just like the rich fool of Luke 12:16-21, Nebuchadnezzar's contented prosperity was shattered when the real world of the heavens interrupted his life (verses 4-5).

On this occasion Nebuchadnezzar told the contents of the dream to his wise advisers (verse 7), though they were unable to make sense of it. Daniel, again, was enabled to give the meaning because "the spirit of the holy gods is in him".

> **NOTE:** Nebuchadnezzar realizes that the Living God is obviously more than one divine person – '*elahh* (Aramaic) – 'gods'. However, it seems clear that the word is used to refer to only one divine being. This same word is used by Ezra many times to refer to the Living God when it is clear that Ezra is not referring to several different gods – e.g. Ezra 5:1-2; 5:11-17; though it is the preferred word used by Artaxerxes in his letter of Ezra 7:15-26. Understanding that the one God is a community of divine people is natural to the follower of Jesus (whether in the Old Testament or New Testament), but both Nebuchadnezzar an Artaxerxes, with their pagan background, may have struggled to know how to speak of this Trinitarian God.

Daniel

Nebuchadnezzar had dreamed of a mighty tree that stretched up to the heavens and across the earth. Creatures from across the earth were able to take shelter in this wonderful tree. However, one of the divine watchers was sent from heaven to trim it right back to the stump. This stump would be bound with iron, drenched with dew and left to live among the animals for seven years.

At first, when Daniel heard this dream, he was 'perplexed' (verse 19) and afraid because he knew that the dream was a judgement against Nebuchadnezzar. Though he had formed a great empire covering so much of the earth, yet he was to be humbled by the Living God, made to live like an animal… if he did not humble himself.

The dream was a warning. A day of judgement was coming for Nebuchadnezzar and he had a year to put his house in order. How would he respond? Would he seek the face of the fourth figure of the fiery furnace? Would he recognize that compared to that Glorious Son of Man, his own kingdom and power were as nothing?

Daniel puts the matter very clearly:

> O king, be pleased to accept my advice: Renounce your sins by doing what is right, and renounce your wickedness by being kind to the oppressed. It may be that then your prosperity will continue. (Verse 18).

This solemn advice is good for us all to hear. We so easily wander through life imagining that all is well with us, that we are safe and secure, that our future is good, that God is pleased with us. The flash of lightning from the heavens can reveal, for a moment, what the darkness of this age conceals. If we really had the eternal life of the Living God then we would be full of kindness to oppressed people, compassion for the widows and orphans, generosity to the poor, practical love for those in need. It is so easy to substitute an abstract 'religion' or 'faith' for this genuine Way, truth and Life of Jesus.

We must flee for our lives to the LORD Jesus, away from the selfish, pointless, empty lives that we lead. We need to run from the tiny vision of life that is obsessed with the fleeting ways and treasures of this passing age and run to the life of self-sacrifice, compassion, service and obedience

that we find in Jesus. Our wealth and status and comfort will drag us down into Hell if we cling onto it rather than let it go to the glory of Jesus.

Nebuchadnezzar was given a stark warning.

He did not heed the warning.

A year went by and then as he was enjoying all his success…

> As the king was walking on the roof of the royal palace of Babylon, he said, "Is not this the great Babylon I have built as the royal residence, by my mighty power and for the glory of my majesty?" The words were still on his lips when a voice came from heaven…
> (verses 29-31)

He had been warned… and the warnings of the Living God are never empty. If like the people of Nineveh in the book of Jonah we respond by turning from our selfish ways and following the Way of the Son of Man, then the judgement may be withheld. However, if we ignore the Living God then the voice from heaven will speak against us too.

Nebuchadnezzar was afflicted with some strange condition that reduced him to the life of an animal for seven years. There have been various attempts to 'diagnose' the specific 'illness' but this does not seem to be very useful. For seven years he grazed grass like a cow, had hair like an eagle's feathers and nails like the claws of bird.

Only when, out of the depths, he cried out to the Most High God was he restored.

His prayer of praise to the Living God is one of the great prayers of the whole Bible:

> His dominion is an eternal dominion; his kingdom endures from generation to generation. All the peoples of the earth are regarded as nothing. He does as he pleases with the powers of heaven and the peoples of the earth. No one can hold back his hand or say to him: "What have you done?"

Can there be a better definition of the almighty power of the LORD God? If we ask how powerful the Living God really is, the best possible answer is simply Daniel 4:35.

Daniel

The restoration of Nebuchadnezzar reminds us of the restoration of Legion in Mark 5:15. Whether Nebuchadnezzar was possessed by evil spirits in the same way, we cannot tell. However, both Legion and Nebuchadnezzar reveal to us what our lives really are if we are cut off, exiled, from the life of God – out of our minds, unclean, less than human, shut out from all true community.

In our pride we may imagine we are safe, yet the Living God will always humble our pride in the end. Whether we are humbled in this life as the LORD so kindly did for Nebuchadnezzar, or whether he simply leaves us to face the irreversible humbling of the last day… there can be no place for pride and selfishness in the life of the eternal God. Everything He does is right and all His ways are just (verse 37).

BookbyBook

Study 2 Bible Questions

Daniel 3:13-30

1. Verses 13-14 – What is so strange about the words of Nebuchadnezzar? Think of the argument in Isaiah 40:9-20.
2. What are the man-made things and ideas that we also serve? What are the golden idols that command our attention?
3. Verse 15 – Is it fair to say that Nebuchadnezzar was an atheist? Does he believe in any god other than his man-made statue?
4. Verses 16-18 – What do Shadrach, Meshach and Abednego believe in order to speak like this? How can they be so fearless when facing such a terrible fate?
5. Verses 19-23 – Why was Nebuchadnezzar so enraged by the words of the young saints?
6. Verses 24-25 – Does it make any difference whether the fourth figure is just a created angel or the Son of God Himself, Jesus the LORD?
7. Verse 26 – What has changed about Nebuchadnezzar?
8. Verses 27 – Why is it important to see that the fire had not harmed them in any way? Why bother noting that there was not even the smell of smoke?
9. Verses 28-30 – What are the most remarkable features of Nebuchadnezzar's praise?

Daniel

Study 2   Further Questions

1. If materialism is idolatry, then how do we break down these idols? What actions might we do in order to show how powerless the gods of money and possessions really are?

2. If we pray to be delivered from suffering or illness and the Living God does not deliver us, then what are we to do? How do we cope with not being delivered from the furnace? Can we still trust and praise even when He does allow us to die?

3. Nebuchadnezzar became like an animal because of his pride. Does human sin always turn us into animals? What does it mean to be a real man or a real woman?

Study 2   Daily Readings

Day 1   Daniel 3:1-12
Day 2   Daniel 3:13-30
Day 3   Daniel 4:1-18
Day 4   Daniel 4:19-37
Day 5   Colossians 3:1-14
Day 6   Colossians 3:15-25
Day 7   Psalm 115

The daily Bible readings are an opportunity to not only read through all of the material in the book under study, but also to read parts of the Bible that relate to the themes and issues that we have been considering. We try to make sure that we receive light from the whole Bible as we think through the key issues each week.

Writings on the wall

Daniel

Study 3 "My God sent His Angel"

Daniel 5-6

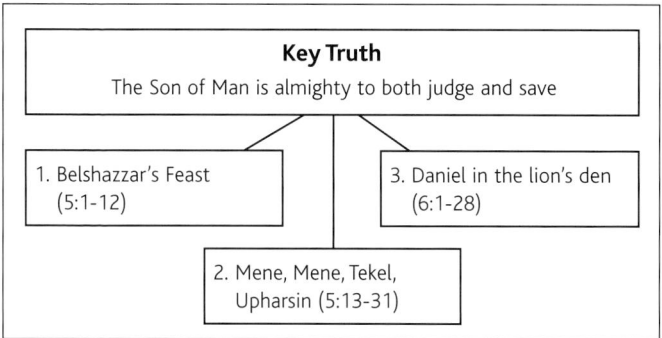

1. Belshazzar's Feast (Chapter 5:1-12)

Chapter 5 of Daniel begins with a new king – Belshazzar. Although he is described as being the 'son' of Nebuchadnezzar, there were other kings on the throne between Nebuchadnezzar and Belshazzar. One of them – Evil-Merodach – is mentioned in Jeremiah 52:31. Just as Jesus is called the 'Son of David' even though many years (many generations) had passed between them, so in this way Belshazzar is called the son of Nebuchadnezzar though Belshazzar was a later descendant.[30]

Belshazzar has forgotten the lessons that the great Nebuchadnezzar had learnt, the lessons that Nebuchadnezzar had gone to so much trouble to record for others to study. Nebuchadnezzar had learned that the LORD God of Israel had to be taken very, very seriously – that He was the One who reigned over the highest heaven and over all that happened on earth (Daniel 4:34-35).

---

[30] There are some who have taken the view that the book of Daniel was written much later than the time of Daniel. The reasoning behind this conclusion is essentially that the book speaks about events and empires that were in Daniel's future. However, when we take the book at face value we see that it does in fact claim to be foretelling future events as well as commenting on contemporary events. If we acknowledge that there really is a Living God who knows the future and sometimes speaks through His prophets about future events... then there is no reason to doubt that the book of Daniel really is what it appears to be!

The very fact of Babylon being drunk when her destruction came upon her was spoken by the prophet Jeremiah (Jeremiah 51:56-7).[31]

Belshazzar had a big drinking party for all his friends. Proverbs 31:4 warns of the dangers of kings drinking wine because the bad decisions they make when drunk can have terrible consequences. That was certainly the case with Belshazzar.

The wine had stripped away his inhibitions and thinking of something new to try, Belshazzar decides to bring out the gold and silver goblets that had been taken from the temple in Jerusalem. Not only does Nebuchadnezzar have many wives but he also has concubines (verse 2), and this hedonistic man wants them all to drink from these sacred cups.

Furthermore, as they drank from these holy goblets, they praised their false gods made by human hands. Once we set ourselves against the Living God, there is no limit to the foolish evil we may fall into. On the windowsill near to my desk, my wife Liz has placed a vase of beautiful cut flowers. Disconnected from the living plant they still look so alive and full of vitality. They may still look like that tomorrow and even the day after that... but by the time we get to this time next week, these flowers will be faded and falling apart. A week after that they will be rotting on the rubbish tip. This is how it is with human beings also. Cut off from the Cosmic Christ Jesus, we may initially look as if we are still flourishing, yet the life is no longer flowing into us. As time goes on, so the dangers of decay and corruption become ever more serious.

We don't use sacred objects from the ancient temple, yet so often we use the sacred gifts that the Living God has given to us in blasphemous ways. In our exile and rebellion we use our gifts and talents, our bodies and our sexuality, our friends and family, the resources of the world around us,

---

31 Notice how the Bible remembers this image of adulterous and drunken Babylon as the great vision of the world awaiting its destruction. Babylon becomes a 'code word' for much more than this ancient city or empire. 'Babylon' means the whole human world in this passing age of darkness and sin. The whole of Revelation chapter 18 is a prophecy of how this whole edifice of human life will collapse – and collapse so quickly. The association of drunkenness is retained from Belshazzar's Feast. Rev 14:3 - "A second angel followed and said, "Fallen! Fallen is Babylon the Great, which made all the nations drink the maddening wine of her adulteries." Yet, in Revelation 16:19-20 Babylon's desire to drunk wine is judged as she is forced to drink the cup of God's wrath. In Revelation 17:5-6 Babylon is drunk not simply on wine but on the blood of the saints who she has murdered.

Daniel

using all these things in sacrilegious ways that provoke the anger of the Most Holy God.

Belshazzar was out of control, alienated from the life of God, he no longer had any fear of God and was racing headlong into the brick wall of eternal judgement. The Son of Man who had protected His saints in the hot furnace, had now come to write His judgement against Belshazzar. As the divine graffiti was inscribed on the wall, Belshazzar knew that this LORD God was not like the impotent gods of human creation.

The "wise men" of the empire are called for and once again fail to deliver any wisdom. However, the queen remembered Daniel. Unlike Belshazzar she remembered the lessons in reality that Nebuchadnezzar had learned and she told Belshazzar to called for Daniel – "the Spirit of God is in him" (verse 11).

Life seems to go on uninterrupted, day after day in this present age of the world. People come and go, evil prospers and the poor and vulnerable are left at the bottom of the pile. The powerful and wealthy seem to have everything, acting with impunity. We go through the round of each day, more concerned for our own comfort and success than the glory of God. Yet, a day has been set by the Father when everything will be put right – Justice Day, when Jesus appears and the kingdom of the Living God pushes aside once and for all the kingdoms of this earth. The divine/human hand, breaking in like a meteor from the heavens, wrote the verdict that stands over the world.

2. Mene, Mene, Tekel, Upharsin (Chapter 5:13-31)

The hand that writes on the wall is described as a "human hand". Whose hand is it? We have already seen the rest of this person walking in the furnace and in Daniel chapter 7 we will see Him receiving all power and authority from the Ancient of Days.[32]

Belshazzar is so desperate to find out what the divine graffiti said that he makes extravagant promises to Daniel – verse 16. Although this may have

---

32 In one sense it is strange to call this a 'human hand' because it is the original hand that all human hands were copied from! We were created as copies or images of this Eternal Son of Man. Yet, the wonder of Christmas is that the original becomes a copy in order to restore the copies back to the original.

sounded a great deal, his kingdom was about to fall, as all human kingdoms do. When Jesus warns us to store up treasure in heaven where real value lies, He is telling us to weigh and assess all these earthly treasures in the divine scales. Can we be bought by earthly treasure? As we read the end of Daniel chapter 5 we can see how fleeting is the power and glory of the kings of the earth.

Verse 17 – "Daniel answered the king, 'You may keep your gifts for yourself…'"

When we face the temptations of power and status and influence and money, it is so very important that we have Daniel's attitude to earthly glory. So often the church has climbed into bed with political and cultural power, looking for influence and relevance. Speaking and living out the kingdom of the Son of Man in all its counter-cultural power always brings so much more deep change in society and culture.

In interpreting the message from the Son of Man Daniel goes back to the basic issues that Nebuchadnezzar had learned. The basis of all human power lies in the power of the Most High God. He appoints the leaders of nations as His ministers and He gives them whatever power and authority they have.

The apostle Paul would later pick this up in his letter to the Christians living under a different totalitarian regime, ruled by another emperor with godlike pretensions. Romans 13:1 – "Everyone must submit himself to the governing authorities, for there is no authority except that which God has established. The authorities that exist have been established by God."

Remember that both the words of Daniel and the words of Paul were written under very unfavourable political circumstances. They were not speaking of the responsible exercise of carefully defined political power in a liberal democracy, but oppressive systems that were hostile to the claims of the kingdom of the heavens.

As followers of Jesus we are not permitted to take violence or vengeance into our hands. We have to submit to the political authorities that have been given the authority to administer law and order under the ultimate power of the Most High God. Whether they fulfil their role or rebel against it, we may speak with prophetic truth and work for the kingdom of Jesus under their rule. We may wrestle with these principalities and powers, yet we must always remember that they receive their power from the Most High God. He is the One who raises them up and when we cry to Him, he is the One who can bring them down.

Notice the careful parallel in verses 18-21 between the power that Nebuchadnezzar was given over all the peoples, and then the power that the Most High God exercised over Nebuchadnezzar. Sandwiched between verse 18 and verses 20-21 comes verse 19.

Nebuchadnezzar over the nations – verse 19	The Most High over Nebuchadnezzar – verses 18, 20-21
	18 O king, the Most High God gave your father Nebuchadnezzar sovereignty and greatness and glory and splendor.
19 Because of the high position he gave him, all the peoples and nations and men of every language dreaded and feared him. Those the king wanted to put to death, he put to death; those he wanted to spare, he spared; those he wanted to promote, he promoted; and those he wanted to humble, he humbled.	
	20 But when his heart became arrogant and hardened with pride, he was deposed from his royal throne and stripped of his glory. 21 He was driven away from people and given the mind of an animal; he lived with the wild donkeys and ate grass like cattle; and his body was drenched with the dew of heaven, until he acknowledged that the Most High God is sovereign over the kingdoms of men and sets over them anyone he wishes.

The Most High God who gave him his power humbled Nebuchadnezzar and he came to acknowledge that the Living God can do as He pleases with everything in heaven and on earth.

However, even though Belshazzar had the wonderful record of all this from Nebuchadnezzar himself, yet he had set himself up against the Lord of heaven (verse 23). The LORD God is so amazingly patient and gentle; so He waited and allowed Belshazzar time to think again, time to repent, time to learn the lessons of his ancestor. However, when his arrogance was so grave that he no longer had the slightest respect for the holy things of the Living God then his judgement burst upon him.

> "You praised the gods of silver and gold, of bronze, iron, wood and stone, which cannot see or hear or understand. But you did not honour the God who holds in His hand your life and all your ways." (verse 23).

We must all meditate on this fearsome verdict, especially those of us who live in cultures that still worship mindless, man-made gods of silver and gold. Those of us who so often worship money and possessions, looking to them for refreshment when we get home in the evening or joy when we are down, need to see that our hearts are exposed by this – we will be found wanting in the divine scales.

The Aramaic words on the wall spell out the verdict for Belshazzar. They are economic words indicating that his bill is ready to be paid but he does not have the money to pay the bill, therefore his kingdom must be divided.

Mene – numbered; added up. The bill is calculated and the debt assessed.
Tekel – weighed. The wallet is weighed against the bill.
Peres – divided. There are severe consequences for non-payment.

The word *Peres* has two ideas within it, picked up by Daniel. It could come from the root meaning 'to divide' but can also be a reference to the Persians

One of the key Biblical metaphors describing our exile and rebellion against the Living God revolves around the idea of debt. We could imagine someone staying at a hotel. They stay in the hotel as if everything all belonged to them, as if it was all their private property for their own use and enjoyment. They eat all the food, drink all they desire,

Daniel

use all the facilities and take advantage of the different services. Yet, the moment of 'check-out' inevitably comes and there is a bill to pay. That is the moment when it becomes clear that it all belongs to someone else and there is a heavy price to pay for the way we have lived.

If we cannot pay for our stay in the universe, if we are not guests of the owner, then it is no surprise that we will be thrown outside.

Rembrandt's amazing painting, *Belshazzar's Feast*, is a wonderful image. The shock on Belshazzar's face as he sees the writing is reflected on the faces of the guests as they look at him. That very night his soul was required of him, and he was not ready. Did the guests see their own mortality in that moment as they saw reality reflected on Belshazzar's face?

Still reeling in shock, Belshazzar gives his reward to Daniel (verse 29), but that very night he is killed as the mighty Persian Empire invaded and brought an end to the great Babylonian empire.

Jeremiah 51 prophesied how the Babylonian empire would fall, possibly even that she would be destroyed in a single day. (Jeremiah 51:1-2)

All the mighty empires (and republics, media networks, multinational companies) of the world are all under the rule of the Living God. We can wrestle against them and work for the Divine Kingdom right among them, confident in the knowledge that the stone that became a mountain is still rolling, still knocking down every power that stands against it.

3. Daniel in the lion's den (Chapter 6:1-28)

Nebuchadnezzar had marked the high point of the Babylonian Empire and since his death there had been a shift of power towards the east.[33]

To the east of Babylon, Cyrus the Great (600-530 BC) united the different factions and formed a powerful new empire, defeating the Medes, the Lydians and then the Babylonians in 539 BC. Darius was probably one of his senior generals, with a Mede background, and he administered the defeated Babylonian empire under the overall rule of Cyrus.[34]

---

33 From Nebuchadnezzar through Awil-Marduk (*Evil-Merodach*) and Nabonidus the Babylonian Empire limped into the final years with Belshazzar who ruled under Nabonidus.

34 Cyrus' sons struggled to rule after him until Darius (549-486 BC) (married to one of Cyrus' daughters) took control of the Persian Empire in 522 BC.

So, Daniel chapter 5 ends with Darius the Mede taking control of the defeated Babylonian empire, needing skilled administrators to integrate this conquered territory into Cyrus' great Persian Empire.

The book of Daniel is filled with deep symbolism. The number 12 is associated with kingdoms and government, which is why there are 12 tribes of Israel, 12 apostles and 12 foundations in the city of God.[35] In this same way Darius organises his domain under the control of 120 satraps (12 times 10).

Three top administrators oversaw the 120 satraps: Daniel plus two others. Daniel was so gifted at his work that Darius planned to put him in overall charge of the whole kingdom. This created deep jealousy among the other administrators and the satraps: Daniel was a foreigner who kept himself culturally distinct. How could he be preferred above those who treated the kingdom as their ultimate desire and destiny?

As followers of Jesus we do all our work as if we were working for Jesus Himself. We care for those who are working for us just as if Jesus Himself were working for us. Others may treat their work carelessly or ruthlessly, yet the Christian is able to bring the glory of Jesus into all their work, whether we serve at the highest level like Daniel or at the very lowest level like Onesimus – Ephesians 6:5-9.

This is how Daniel did his work and because of this the LORD Jesus could trust him with great responsibility. As Daniel worked like that his work was of the very highest standard and his enemies could find no evidence of corruption or mistakes – verse 4. So, verse 5:

> Finally these men said, "We will never find any basis for charges against this man Daniel unless it has something to do with the law of his God."

King Darius, like us all, was very susceptible to pride. The satraps and administrators knew that Darius had delusions of grandeur, aspirations to

---

35 This is also why time is divided up around the number 12. Even those cultures that rebel against the Living God still want to feel that time and history is ordered and governed. We generally prefer a clock face with the 12 numbers visible to us, rather than a digital readout so that we are aware of the government of time. Even the way the year is organized into 12 months and 12 signs of the zodiac – all these patterns point to the deep symbolic structures in the universe.

Daniel

divinity. This is in every human heart but it becomes ever closer to the surface the more power we get.

So, in verses 6-9 they speak to Darius as if he were a god, as if everybody ought to acknowledge him as a god, as if for a time no other god should eclipse his divine majesty! Not only should Darius live forever (verse 6) but he must take the highest place above every god or man (verse 7). The penalty for rejecting this blasphemy was to be thrown to the lions.

Lions are the most ferocious of all creatures in this fallen world. In Genesis 49:9; Numbers 23:24, 24:9 and Deut 33:20, the lion is so violent and deadly that nobody would dare to provoke a lion. Proverbs 30:29-31 indicates that the lion is the king of all beasts, frightened of nothing. To indicate the miraculous strength and courage of Samson, filled with the Spirit of the Living God, we are told how he was able to deal with a lion with an even greater ferocity (Judges 14:5). That same theme occurs with David (1 Samuel 17:34-36) and Benaiah (2 Samuel 23:20). Only the power of the Living God can overcome a lion. Throughout Psalms and Proverbs the power of the lion is held up time and time again.

To be thrown to the lions is to face certain death – "like a lion among the beasts of the forest, like a young lion among flocks of sheep, which mauls and mangles as it goes, and no one can rescue" (Micah 5:8).

The devil himself revels in the violent, destructive ferocity of the lion, prowling around as an imitation (1 Peter 5:8).

The enemies of Daniel want to ensure that Daniel is killed with no possibility of rescue. Perhaps they heard how Daniel's friends survived the hot furnace, but surely there is no way to survive for even one second in a pit of lions!

Perhaps they realised that Darius might regret this universal decree before very long, so they made sure that it was put in writing to prevent it being cancelled.[36]

What did Daniel think as he went home after reading the decree (verse 10)? It must have been a very thoughtful walk. His daily practice had always been to pray three times a day facing Jerusalem, with the windows open. What should he do now?

---

36 It seems that (verse 8) once the decree was written down and published, it was impossible to revoke even for the king himself.

He could not give up prayer for a month as if Darius really did have the power to prevent the saints from speaking to their Father in heaven. Perhaps it might be better to keep praying, but to at least close the windows. Yet, his enemies clearly knew what Daniel did at those three times of the day. If Daniel closed the windows they would know what was going on and they would also know that Daniel was trying to hide the fact. To be faithful to the Son of Man, to show that he feared the Living God more than mere human beings, Daniel had not option but to continue as he had before.

> 1 Peter 3:13-15 – "Who is going to harm you if you are eager to do good? But even if you should suffer for what is right, you are blessed. "Do not fear what they fear; do not be frightened." But in your hearts set apart Christ as Lord."

The satraps and administrators burst in on Daniel (verse 11) and reported the 'offence' to Darius who was very upset (verse 14). He realised how the whole thing had been a cunning trick and that both he and Daniel were their victims. It is strange that as a god-man who was the object of prayer for the whole kingdom, he was unable to rescue Daniel no matter how hard he tried.

When the night time came, and all hope seemed to be gone, Darius had to carry out the decree. However, the king looked to the true God who is served not just for 30 days but continually – "The king said to Daniel, "May your God, whom you serve continually, rescue you!" (verse 16).

From every human viewpoint it was hopeless. Not only was Daniel thrown to the lions but the mouth of the lion's den was sealed over to prevent any help getting to Daniel – verse 17. Furthermore, the lion is an unclean animal (Leviticus 11:27) and their den would have been littered with carcasses and blood. If Daniel was trying to keep this law of the Living God, then there could hardly have been a more unclean way of dying. It is almost as if his enemies not only wanted Daniel discredited before the world but also before his God.

It was a sleepless night for Darius, yet as soon as the sun rose he rushed down to see if there was a God who could rescue those who serve Him – verse 20.

Daniel

Daniel's answer is amazing – verse 22 – "My God sent His Angel, and he shut the mouths of the lions. They have not hurt me, because I was found innocent in his sight. Nor have I ever done any wrong before you, O king."

The Angel of the Living God came to spend the night with Daniel in the lion's den. Just as Shadrach, Meshach and Abednego had enjoyed His fellowship in the hot furnace, so too Daniel knew what it was to know Christ and the fellowship of His sufferings.

What a glorious night Daniel must have enjoyed in worst place in the kingdom, while the great king, in the most luxurious place in the kingdom, had been tormented all night!

There is a deep wonder here. If lions are now the most ferocious and fearless of all the beasts in this fallen age, yet the LORD Jesus has different plans for them. In His presence, in His New Creation future, the lion is an affectionate kitten, as harmless and friendly as a lamb.

Isaiah 11 begins with a glorious prophecy of the Coming Messiah and the marvellous renewed creation He will bring about. Full of the Spirit, Christ Jesus will bring His reign of peace and justice even to the animals.

Even now many people keep small cats as pets. My brother-in-law loves them and seems to have about a dozen of them. These predators of the night, these creatures of fang and claw, seem peaceful and harmless as he holds them. If even we human beings can somewhat tame these small animals, then what wonders of renewal and recreation will happen when the Divine Son of Man tames the whole fallen created order on the Day of His Appearing?

Daniel perhaps glimpsed something of that future glory when he spent the night in the lion's den in the presence of Jesus. Did he sleep peacefully among these giant kittens or was he simply too overwhelmed by the presence of the Son of Man to even close his eyes?

Darius was overjoyed to see that the Living God had saved Daniel. The satraps and administrators were caught in their own traps, bringing terrible destruction not only to themselves but also to their families – verse 24. Once the Angel of God left the lions, they returned to their fallen ferocity with enthusiasm.

We have seen how the decrees of these human kings, whether intended for good or ill, are not able to either resist or bring about the Kingdom of the Son of Man. Nevertheless, it is thrilling to see that Darius commanded all men everywhere to "fear and reverence the God of Daniel" – verse 26. As Nebuchadnezzar had learned, so too did Darius: the Kingdom of the Living God will never end – verse 26. The Divine King is able to do as He pleases in heaven or on earth.

This is how the story of Daniel ends. We are told that Daniel continued to serve in this role right until the first year of the reign of Cyrus – Daniel 1:21. After that Daniel seemed to go into retirement. The rest of the book takes us into the deep and wonderful visions that Daniel had while he was serving under Belshazzar, Darius and Cyrus. Yet, as we will see, all these visions were given to teach this same truth, the truth that Darius states in such clear and simple terms.

The Kingdom of the Son of Man is above and before and beyond all the passing kingdoms and powers of this present age. His kingdom will never end and the servants of His kingdom look ahead to the day when His rule will overwhelm the whole creation in age of resurrection and righteousness.

Daniel

Study 3 Bible Questions

Daniel 6:1-10

1. Verses 1-2 – How could Daniel work in such a senior position for a godless, pagan nation? How can a believer work for such an ungodly system?

2. Verse 3 – How did Daniel come to have such exceptional abilities? (Remember chapter 1:15-20).

3. Verses 3-4 – Why is it so important for our work to be of the highest level we can possibly achieve? If the 'praise of men' is of no final value, why should we work so hard to show integrity and excellence in our work?

4. Verse 5 – Daniel could not be attacked professionally, so he had to be attacked in terms of his commitment to the LORD God. How might this happen today? How do people try to upset or provoke us concerning our love for Jesus?

5. Verses 6-9 – What does this speech tell us about the enemies of Daniel? Is their speech honest or deceitful?

6. Verse 10 – Why did Daniel continue to pray three times a day even when he knew about the decree?

7. When is it right to come into conflict with the law and when is it right to avoid the conflict? In a democracy do we also have the added responsibility of speaking out about the laws that might create such conflicts?

Study 3 Further Questions

1. Belshazzar's Feast has inspired a variety of works of art, whether in music or visual arts. How useful are these works? Do they draw us deeper into the stories, bringing them to life? Or do they distract us away from the specific Biblical message?

2. Given that the LORD God is a graffiti artist, how important is street art? When some of the most powerful comments on our society come from street art, shouldn't it be given the same level of respect as more traditional forms of art? Should local councils provide urban spaces for this kind of art? How is it best preserved?

3. Are there any careers that a Christian could not ever pursue, no matter how faithfully they held onto their heavenly citizenship?

Daniel

Study 3	Daily Readings
Day 1	Daniel 5:1-12
Day 2	Daniel 5:13-30
Day 3	Matthew 25:31-46
Day 4	Daniel 6:1-12
Day 5	Daniel 6:13-28
Day 6	Isaiah 11:1-9
Day 7	Isaiah 65:17-25

The daily Bible readings are an opportunity to not only read through all of the material in the book under study, but also to read parts of the Bible that relate to the themes and issues that we have been considering. We try to make sure that we receive light from the whole Bible as we think through the key issues each week.

The taller they are

Daniel

Study 4 "One like the Son of Man"

Daniel 7-8

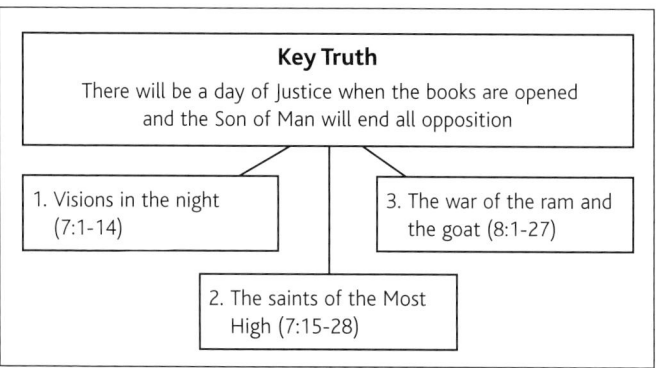

1. Visions in the night (Chapter 7:1-14)

The first six chapters of the book of Daniel set out the major biographical features of the life of Daniel, from his arrival in Babylon as a young man right through to his service as a senior administrator into his old age. In those first chapters the focus stays on the dreams that other people had, dreams that Daniel was given the ability to interpret.

However, in the rest of the book of Daniel we discover that Daniel too had been given dreams and visions. The second six chapters of the book of Daniel go back through his life picking out various visions that Daniel had while working as a senior civil servant.

		Main Theme of Vision	Historical Date	When in Daniel's life
1	Daniel 7	The Four Beasts	Belshazzar Year 1	Between Daniel 4 & 5
2	Daniel 8	A Ram and A Goat	Belshazzar Year 3	Between Daniel 4 & 5
3	Daniel 9	Seventy Sevens	Darius Year 1	Daniel 6
4	Daniel 10-12	All of Human History	Cyrus Year 3	Possibly after his retirement

So, Daniel chapter 7 begins by taking us back to events in the life of Daniel that happened sometime after the end of the reign of Nebuchadnezzar when Belshazzar had come to power. We have seen the character of Belshazzar and the terrible judgement that he brought upon himself and his kingdom, but perhaps the early days of his reign were filled with optimism or just uncertainty.

What would the future hold?

Was there any future for the church of the Living God in the troubling times to come?

Perhaps some thought that there were only good times ahead, that the prophecies of restoration from Isaiah, Jeremiah and Ezekiel meant that it was going to be easy from now on. Perhaps Belshazzar was going to bring in a time of security and stability.

How are the saints of the Living God to stand firm among all the nations of the world, as the wheels of world history turn around them?

Matthew Henry, the great Bible commentator of the 18th century, says that this first vision "foretells the revolutions of government in those nations which the church of the Jews, for the following ages, was to be under the influence of." In other words, it was a message to the church concerning all the troubles to come. Daniel had so many concerns about the state of the ancient church, yet in these next chapters he is told not only of general conflict but of two very specific moments when individuals would bring extreme persecution: Antiochus Epiphanes, the Syrian ruler[37]; Vespasian and his son Titus, the Roman leader.[38]

Daniel wrote down these dreams as soon as he awoke – 7:1. He knew enough about the importance of dreams to record the details.

Throughout these dreams we need to be very sensitive to the deep Biblical symbolism of what we read. The book of Daniel has already

---

[37] Antiochus Epiphanes was born around 215 BC and ruled the Seleucid Syrian kingdom from 174-164 BC. He plundered the temple in Jerusalem in 169 BC and then desecrated the temple with pig sacrifices to Zeus in 167 BC.

[38] After a Jewish revolt, Vespasian conquered Jerusalem in 67AD, before his son Titus finally destroyed the temple in 70 AD – just as Jesus Himself had prophesied – Luke 19:41-44.

Daniel

prepared us to appreciate the significance of numbers and symbols. Sometimes Bible readers will become distracted or even obsessed with some of these dreams and visions, not only here but also in the New Testament book of Revelation, because they lose sight of the big picture. They lose their way in the flurry of symbols, when they need to see how the same basic truth may be spoken of in several ways, from several angles.

The basic theme of the vision is revealed right from verses 2-3. As we noted earlier, throughout the Bible the number four indicates the whole world.[39] The presence of the four winds from heaven and the four beasts from the sea show that the vision concerns all of heaven and earth.

The four winds stir up the sea and the four beasts come out of the sea. In the Bible the sea stands for chaos, the Abyss, the world in rebellion. The Bible rejoices in the LORD's ability to control the Red Sea in the Exodus precisely because the sea seems to be so hard to control. The LORD alone is able to set a boundary for the sea beyond which it will not dare to cross – Jeremiah 5:22 – "Should you not fear me?" declares the LORD. "Should you not tremble in my presence? I made the sand a boundary for the sea, an everlasting barrier it cannot cross. The waves may roll, but they cannot prevail; they may roar, but they cannot cross it."[40]

The four winds that blow the sea indicate the chaos unleashed when the princes and powers of the world struggle for power over the nations. Matthew Henry puts this so well:

---

[39] There are four points to the compass: north, south, east and west (Luke 13:29). In Genesis 2:10-11 the river that watered the whole earth split into four great rivers. There are four winds throughout the earth (Jeremiah 49:36; Ezekiel 37:9; Daniel 7:2, 8:8, 11:4; Zechariah 2:6; Matthew 24:31; Mark 13:27; Revelation 7:1). There are four seasons throughout the year (Genesis 8:22; Deuteronomy 11:14). There are four heavenly living creatures (ruling cherubim) who keep watch over the whole earth and give the decisions of the Divine Son of Man (Ezekiel 1:5; Revelation 4:6-8, 5:6-8, 5:14, 6:1, 6:6, 7:11, 14:3, 15:7, 19:4). These four living creatures each have four faces (Ezekiel 1:6, 10, 15; 10:14). The tabernacle represented the whole creation and it was made of four materials (gold, silver, brass and wood).

[40] From Genesis 1:2 we see the same theme as the Living God triumphed over the darkness and chaos as the Light of Jesus shone in the darkness on day 1 of creation. In Mark 4:39 Jesus commands the unruly sea and it instantly obeys Him. In Matthew 1 Jesus is even able to walk calmly on the sea, which is surely a terrifying act of power. Revelation 21:1 reassures us that there will be no sea when the creation is renewed as the eternal home of the Living God.

This represents the contests among princes for empire, and the shakings of the nations by these contests, to which those mighty monarchies, which he was now to have a prospect of, owed their rise. One wind from any point of the compass, if it blow hard, will cause a great commotion in the sea; but what a tumult must needs be raised when the four winds strive for mastery! This is it which the kings of the nations are contending for in their wars, which are as noisy and violent as the battle of the winds... Note, This world is like a stormy tempestuous sea; thanks to the proud ambitious winds that vex it.

So, the vision concerns the chaos and rebellion that will trouble all the earth in the coming years. Each beast had a different nature and brought different kinds of trouble, yet the fourth beast was the most terrible.

Beast	Reference	Nature and Power	Kingdom
Lion	Daniel 7:4	Has the heart of a man	Babylon
Bear	Daniel 7:5	Eats flesh	Persia
Leopard	Daniel 7:6	Authority to rule	Greece
Horned Beast	Daniel 7:7-8	Crushes and devours	Rome? All human kingdoms?

These are the most ferocious and dangerous beasts in the Bible. It is terrifying to think that the world might lie under the power of such creatures.

When describing the severity of His judgement the LORD says "I will come upon them like a lion, like a leopard I will lurk by the path. Like a bear robbed of her cubs, I will attack them and rip them open. Like a lion I will devour them; a wild animal will tear them apart" (Hosea 13:7-8). There can be no more hopeless case than to be at the mercy of a lion, a leopard and a bear.

It seems as if the future of world history is as bad as it could possibly be, but then it gets even worse with the fourth beast. It is the same creature that the apostle John would later see coming out of the sea under the command of Satan, the ancient dragon – see Revelation chapter 13.

Daniel

The four beasts are four kingdoms from world history. We may well be thinking here of the Babylonian empire (which was coming to end with Belshazzar) symbolised by the lion; the Persian empire like a viscous bear; the Greek empire like a leopard with extensive ruling authority, having four heads reflecting the division of the Greek empire after the death of Alexander[41]; and finally most take the fourth beast to be the Roman empire, with the most extensive authority and severe brutality of all, although others see the fourth beast in different terms.

It is said that the first beast's wings reflected the speed of Nebuchadnezzar's conquests, whereas the loss of the wings and the lion heart reflects the loss of power and courage of his successors. The third beast had four wings, perhaps reflecting the incredible speed of the conquests of Alexander the Great.

It is vital to remember that this vision was given to Daniel long before these nations rose up in world history. We are not talking here of the foresight of the political analyst but the utterly incomprehensible power of the King of Heaven who is the revealer of mysteries.

This fourth beast causes Daniel the most thought. Various attempts have been made to align the ten horns with ten kingdoms within the Roman Empire or ten senators in the Roman senate or ten Roman emperors.[42] Although possible, the deeper solution may be more obvious. The number ten stands for the totality of something, its fullness or entirety. It may be simply that the fourth beast has such complete power on earth. It is a totalitarian regime, demanding complete obedience and allegiance from its citizens or victims.

The camera zooms in on one of the horns of the beast, a king who gains power in this empire and takes a stand of extreme pride and arrogance. Is this a prophecy of Antiochus Epiphanes? The Roman general Vespasian? The Roman Emperor Nero? Adolf Hitler? Some other religious or political leader?[43]

---

41 Antiochus Epiphanes, who is prophesied in great detail in chapter 11 of Daniel, was one of the later rulers of one of the four kingdoms.

42 Still less plausible are attempts to map this chapter onto the narrow concerns of continental Europe at various historical periods, whether concerning the Holy Roman Empire or the modern European Union.

43 A likely candidate may well be the Roman general Vespasian, with his son Titus, who destroyed the temple in Jerusalem in AD 70. Jesus Himself prophesied that destruction of Jerusalem in Luke 19:41-44.

Perhaps we need to view this beast in a much larger sense. This beast represents all the kingdoms of the world. Through the Bible, the beast represents human political power in every age, crushing, devouring and trampling. It is all too human, all too arrogant – verse 8.

It would be so easy to live under these powerful kingdoms and see them as the true meaning and destiny of history. Even in modern times people spoke about the success of the capitalist empire as the 'end of history', assuming that the real meaning of history is to be found in the rise and fall of these human kingdoms and empires. For Daniel especially, working in such a senior position in two of the beasts, the great temptation might have been to get his identity and purpose from the beasts.

The great truth comes in verses 9-14.

First Daniel is shown God the Father in the courts of heaven – verses 9-10.

Second Daniel is shown the defeat of the beasts – verses 11-12.

Third Daniel is shown heaven's champion, Jesus, the Son of Man – verses 13-14.

In verses 9-10 Daniel sees the Ancient of Days seated in the centre of heaven. When the apostle John saw this scene in Revelation chapter 4 he describes it in more detail, but is quite clear that Daniel saw the very same scene. In the very centre of heaven the Father has established His glorious throne[44], surrounded by hundreds of millions of wonderful angelic servants. The river of fire flowing out from His throne maintains His purity and separation.[45] No matter how lonely and outnumbered we might feel, yet as saints of the Most High we are always backed by hundreds of millions of the angelic host of heaven.

The throne room of heaven is a place of business and activity. It is a courtroom – verse 10. Just as Daniel was used to maintaining the endless records of the Babylonian and Persian empires, so he learns that heaven also has detailed records and the kingdoms of the world are all administered from the true 'capital city of the universe'. As Daniel watches the books are opened and judgements are made.

---

44 Notice that His flaming throne has wheels, showing that He can make His presence felt anywhere in the whole creation, even to the exiles in Babylon. Perhaps it is more like a royal chariot than a static seat.

45 In Genesis 3:24 that fire is placed as a barrier to prevent Adam and Eve from returning from exile.

Daniel

Having seen the judgements of heaven made, the scene switches back to the beasts on the earth, specifically to the small boastful horn of the fourth beast. Even as this leader continued to boast[46], the verdict of heaven was executed and the beast, horns and all, was thrown into the blazing fire – verse 11. The same scene is recorded for us in more detail by the apostle John, in Revelation 19:19-20:[47]

In Revelation 13:4 the worshippers of the beast give a defiant challenge: "who is able to make war against the beast?" and the same question might be asked in Daniel 7. If the verdict of heaven was given, who could possibly carry this out? Who is the rider on the white horse? Who has the strength and authority to stand against the mighty kingdoms of the world to judge them and establish the kingdom of the Living God?

Daniel 7:13-14 is surely one of the most thrilling parts of the whole Bible: a part of Scripture that was especially treasured by Jesus of Nazareth Himself. More than any other title, this is how Jesus saw Himself.[48]

> In my vision at night I looked, and there before me was one like a Son of Man, coming with the clouds of heaven. He approached the Ancient of Days and was led into his presence. He was given authority, glory and sovereign power; all peoples, nations and men of every language worshiped him. His dominion is an everlasting dominion that will not pass away, and his kingdom is one that will never be destroyed.

The unapproachable Ancient of Days is approached by the Son of Man![49] The Ancient of Days has an equal who can carry out all His judgements.

---

46 See Revelation 13:5-6

47 To worship the beast simply means to continue on the broad road of destruction. We worship the beast if we are part of the world, investing in the treasures and values of the world, seeking the comfort and identity that the world gives.

48 Matt 8:20; 9:6; 10:23; 11:19; 12:8, 32, 40; 13:37, 41; 16:13, 27-28; 17:9, 12, 22; 19:28; 20:18, 28; 24:27, 30, 37, 39, 44; 25:31; 26:2, 24, 45, 64; Mark 2:10, 28; 8:31, 38; 9:9, 12, 31; 10:33, 45; 13:26; 14:21, 41, 62; Luke 5:24; 6:5, 22; 7:34; 9:22, 26, 44, 58; 11:30; 12:8, 10, 40; 17:22, 24, 26, 30; 18:8, 31; 19:10; 21:27, 36; 22:22, 48, 69; 24:7; John 1:51; 3:13-14; 5:27; 6:27, 53, 62; 8:28; 9:35; 12:23, 34; 13:31

49 Does this vision refer to the ascension of Jesus when He returned to the throne of heaven after defeating the world, the flesh and the devil at His Cross and Resurrection? Does it refer to the incarnation as some think? Or perhaps it describes the place of the Son of Man in the eternal divine counsels, able to come and go freely to The Ancient of Days, carrying out His will in all matters. Whether it refers to one specific moment in the courts of heaven or the general status of Jesus in the Trinity, the conclusion is clear.

The authority, worship and glory of the Ancient of Days are given to the Son of Man. We can understand why the Pharisees and teachers of the Law reacted so strongly when Jesus constantly revealed Himself to be the Son of Man of Daniel 7.[50] The One Living God is not the Ancient of Days alone, but the Ancient of Days with the Son of Man, together in the unity of the Spirit. The Three together exercise their irresistible authority and righteous rule as the Divine Monarchy.[51]

The kingdom of *heaven* is specifically the kingdom of the *Son of Man*.[52]

The kingdoms of the earth arise from the sea, from the chaos and rebellion, whereas the kingdom of Christ comes down from heaven, from the eternal glory and order of the Ancient of Days.

The kingdoms of this passing age come and go. They each have their own passing glory and their own problems. They battle with each other to be an everlasting dominion and yet they are all the beast of Revelation 13 or the beasts of Daniel 7, all doomed to fall before the Divine kingdom that will never be destroyed. They all may plot against Christ Jesus, but He laughs at them. Enthroned in heaven with all divine power and authority, their rebellious plots and arrogant claims to independence are powerless.[53]

2. The saints of the Most High (Chapter 7:15-28)

In these next verses we learn that the Son of Man shares His life and kingdom with His special people, His saints.

---

50 Sometimes people speak of the 'Son of Man' title as if it meant 'a son of human beings', as if it emphasised the humanity of Jesus. In fact, the very opposite is true! The Son of Man title emphasises the undiluted divinity of Jesus more than any other. It is very useful to study the reactions of the theologians of Jesus' day in the gospels when Jesus refers to Himself as the Son of Man. The Son of Man is the Divine Ruler who is the perfect equal of the Ancient of Days, the One who shares His throne and His glory.

51 The word 'monarchy' indicates the rule of One. The rule of the Divine Three is a monarchy, because they are not three separate gods who happen to work together. No, the Three are One. Together, from the Father, through the Son, in the power of the Spirit they rule as One.

52 In Matthew 8:20 we read some remarkable words from Jesus - "Foxes have holes and birds of the air have nests, but the Son of Man has no place to lay his head." When we think of who He really is, with all authority, glory and power, why would He live in such humility? How can the highest power in the universe come to serve us in such poverty? This is true glory.

53 Psalm 2:1-6

Daniel

When we bow before King Jesus, calling out to Him, He will save us and lead us into His everlasting reign of justice and compassion. Furthermore, in His kingdom we are not mere slaves or subjects. No! We reign with the Son of Man, invited to sit with Him on His throne by the side of the Ancient of Days. What the hundreds of millions of angels can only dream of, we are free to do: speak with the Ancient of Days and the Son of Man, as members of the divine royal family!

Daniel wanted to have a deeper understanding of all that he had seen and so enquired from one of the heavenly host – verses 15-16.[54] The general summary is given in verses 17 and 18: the four beasts are the kingdoms of the earth yet "the saints of the Most High will receive The Kingdom and will possess it for ever – yes, for ever and ever."

Notice how the angel emphasises how the saints have the certainty of a resurrection future in the Father's Kingdom. It is almost as if Daniel's amazement was obvious and the angel had to repeat the guaranteed promise.

Daniel was most concerned about the fourth beast. It seemed to be different from the others and its power was not confined to one geographical area but covered the whole earth – verse 23. In the statue of chapter two, iron and bronze belonged to two separate kingdoms, but here they are all mixed into the one terrible beast. It had ten horns, showing how it seemed to have complete power.[55] More frightening of all, in its final form it had eight horns (verse 20) – as if it were making the terrifying and arrogant claim to be the kingdom of the new creation, the everlasting kingdom.

Eight is the number of new creation throughout the Bible. Jesus Himself rose from the dead on the eighth day, the first day of the new week. The final festival of the Levitical feasts, the feast of tents when they would have looked forward to the city with foundations[56], was an eight day

---

54 The answer given is of such depth and wisdom that we suspect that Daniel was speaking to one of the Watchers, the four living creatures that personally attend the Son of Man – see Ezekiel chapter 1.

55 Consider how the Ten Commandments embody the whole of the Law of Moses or how Daniel was tested for ten days in Daniel chapter 1. Suffering for ten days means that it will end on death according to Revelation 2:10.

56 See Hebrews 11:8-16

feast. Circumcision, which was a sign of new birth and new creation (see Colossians 2:9-12) occurred on the eighth day.

So, when this fourth beast not only claims to have total power (ten horns) but also to be the kingdom of the everlasting future (eight horns), then we can understand why Daniel was so alarmed at this.

The small horn is the figurehead for the beast that fights against the church of the Living God – verse 21. Down through history, and certainly in the experience of Daniel, the nations make war against the saints, the church of Jesus Christ.[57] Whether we think of the total annihilation planned by Haman in the book of Esther or the tyranny of Egypt in the opening chapters of Exodus the story of war against the saints is the same. Whether the open warfare of the Amalekites back in Exodus 17 or the more subtle campaign against Nehemiah, the world will always try to get rid of church. This war might come from religious leaders as Paul experienced in the book of Acts or directly from the kings and emperors. As we look down through history, the fourth beast, as the embodiment of all the empires and kingdoms of this passing age, has made war against the saints, killing so many with ruthless cruelty – verse 21.[58]

The arrogance of the earthly kingdoms is staggering. Not only do they persecute the saints, but they speak against the Living God, rebelling against His laws – verse 25. The worldly kingdoms and empires imagine that they can change or resist what the courts of heaven have decreed for them.

The saints are handed over to the beast for "a time, times and half a time" – verse 25. A 'time' may be one year. 'Times' may refer to two years and 'half a time' may be 6 months. Therefore, the saints will be handed

---

57 Matthew Henry makes the very wise comment: "Whether we understand the fourth beast to signify the Syrian empire, or the Roman, or the former as the figure of the latter, it is plain that these verses are intended for the comfort and support of the people of God in reference to the persecutions they were likely to sustain both from the one and from the other, and from all their proud enemies in every age..."

58 Even if we identify the small horn as Antiochus or Vespasian (each of whom brought three and half years of misery to Jerusalem), yet this vision has profound relevance to the church in every age, in every part of the world. History is filled with other figures who try to destroy the church and bring unbearable suffering on the Body of Christ.

over to this fourth beast for three and a half years. We get this same time measurement in Daniel 12:7 and Revelation 12:14 (and see also Revelation 11:9-11). It can appear as 42 months, as in Revelation 11:2 or even as 1260 days, as in Revelation 11:3 and 12:6. What does it refer to? On the one hand this seems to be a short time and yet in the context it seems to symbolise the whole of history with the saints constantly being persecuted by the world.

Perhaps the first thing to note is that basic measurement of time in the Bible is the week (Genesis 1:1-2:3; Exodus 20:8-11) – seven 'times'.[59] The fact that the time of persecution lasts half this long indicates that the persecution of the kingdoms of the world is temporary, passing, and momentary.[60] It is almost as if the LORD God were saying, "in half the time in took to make the world, it will all be over!" However unbearable it may seem for the saints at times, yet the LORD God cares for us and will never allow His church to perish from the world. This time of trial will seem so short when the day of eternity comes.

As we think of this period of 3 and a half 'times' we are taken back to the life of the great prophet Elijah when he was also pursued by human kings and ungodly nations. Both Jesus and James emphasise that this period lasted for three and half years.[61]

> Luke 4:25 – "I assure you that there were many widows in Israel in Elijah's time, when the sky was shut for three and a half years and there was a severe famine throughout the land."

> James 5:17 – "Elijah was a man just like us. He prayed earnestly that it would not rain, and it did not rain on the land for three and a half years."

---

59 Note how Jacob serves for seven years (Genesis 29:18-20); how the seven years of plenty are replaced by seven years of famine (Genesis 41:26-29); debts had to cancelled every seven years (Deut 15:1) etc.

60 We might note that In Daniel 9:27 the troubled times occur "in the middle of the seven", which also indicates a period of three and a half.

61 1 Kings 18:1 suggests that the rain came after three years, yet the rain was withheld for three and a half years. We need to bear in mind that the rain would come in the early season and then again in the autumn (Deut 11:14; Job 29:23; Prov 16:15; Jer 3:3; Joel 2:23; Zech 10:1; James 5:7). As we read through the events of 1 Kings 17-18 it seems six months after the early rain, everyone was expecting the latter rain, but the LORD withheld the rain for an additional three years.

For three and a half years the land was under the judgement of the LORD God yet the nations rebelled against Him and persecuted Elijah and the other saints. Elijah found it so hard that he wondered if he was the only faithful one left.[62] It may have felt as if all hope was lost, that the arrogant beast was in control. Yet the LORD God had 7,000 who had not bowed the knee to Baal and the mighty judgement and victory of Carmel was at hand.

The church's time of trial in this passing age can seem so long to us. We cry our 'how long O Lord?' yet, just as in Elijah's life, it is a short time and the LORD God is in control. This time of suffering and opposition is only for 'three and a half years' – half of the complete time (a 'week' of time).

Although this story of the beast's war against the church has gone on this way for so long, it is not the final chapter. Though each day so many of the saints are crushed beneath its iron and bronze claws, yet the Ancient of Days has given judgement in favour of the saints, the citizens of His own Kingdom, and they will possess that glorious everlasting kingdom – Daniel 7:26-27.

3. The war of the ram and the goat (Chapter 8:1-27)

How can we know who the real god is? How is it possible to sift between the different religions and the different gods? Many assume that it is all just a matter of opinion and where we were born. However, the Living God sets a real test for any of the religions and gods that would claim to be real. Isaiah 41:21-24.

Two years after that first mighty vision, Daniel has another vision concerning the nations – around 550BC. This time there are two beasts fighting one another: a ram and a goat. The vision begins in a remarkable way, with Daniel at a place that in his day was unimportant but which was destined to be the great central citadel of the Persian Empire, the centre of Persian power according to Nehemiah chapter 1 and Esther chapter 1. In other words, the vision already assumes that the Babylonian Empire has come to an end and the next Empire has taken its place: the golden head has gone and now it is the time of the silver chest (Daniel

---

62 1 Kings 19:10

Daniel

chapter 2); the lion-like beast has fallen and now the bear has arrived (Daniel chapter 7).

Daniel is given a vision of the two kingdoms that would dominate his region of the world for the next generations: the Persian Empire and the Greek empire. The Living God wanted to make it clear to His saints that He really is over all the nations: He knows the future; He raises up nations and He brings them down again. The nations may believe themselves to be masters of their own destiny, but their destiny is as easily known to the Living God as a contest between a goat and a ram.

Initially Daniel sees a ram with two horns charging to the north, south and west. Its two horns were unequal length, because the union of the Medes and the Persians was an unequal alliance (see verse 20). This new empire would attack its neighbours to the north, south and west, enjoying great success in these ventures – verses 3-4.

Nevertheless, a goat would challenge from the west – verse 5. With one mighty horn (presumably Alexander the Great), the Greek empire (verse 21) would make extremely rapid progress in its eastward push (verse 5). As the goat easily defeated the ram, so the Greek empire easily conquered the Persian empire. Just as the one great horn of the goat was replaced by four lesser horns (verses 8, 21-22), so after the death of Alexander the Great, the Greek empire was divided up into four sub-kingdoms. As a small horn grew up [63] from the four to cause serious trouble for 'The Beautiful Land' (verses 9-12, 23-25), challenging the 'Prince of the host', so Antiochus Epiphanes brought destruction and sacrilege to the temple in Jerusalem.[64] Though he had taken his stand against Jesus Christ (verse 25) 2 Maccabees chapter 9:5-10 claims that he died in a terrible way – 'not by human power'. It is said that from the

---

63 In the vision of chapter 7 the small horn grew up from the fourth beast (7:8), but here it is the goat (corresponding to the bear beast of chapter 7) that has the small horn. Each kingdom and empire of world history produces key figures that may oppose the church of the Living God. The horns come and go, but the church remains. If we consider 2 Thessalonians 2:1-11, it may well be that there is yet to be another 'small horn' to cause global trouble for the church.

64 It is said that in 168BC he set up an altar to Zeus in the Temple in Jerusalem and offered pig sacrifices to Zeus. It is hard to imagine a more offensive course of action. We can understand how important it was for the ancient church to have been prepared for these terrible events through Daniel's prophecy.

period of rebellion at the temple to the time of its restoration was exactly the 2,300 days predicted in verse 14.[65]

So accurate are these prophecies that many people assume that they must have been written after the events! The Hebrew Scriptures are packed with detailed predictions of the Messiah, Jesus. Did the Living God give so many precise and detailed predictions of these historical events concerning Persia and Greece to strengthen the church's confidence in the much more important prophecies of Jesus? After studying Daniel chapter 8 we can be in no doubt that the Living God is the Great King above all the little kings, and all the future is laid out before Him as if it were already past.

---

65 See for example the whole Bible commentary of Jameson, Fausset & Brown, speaking of the 2300 days - "Six years and a hundred ten days. This includes not only the three and a half years during which the daily sacrifice was forbidden by Antiochus (JOSEPHUS, Wars of the Jews), but the whole series of events whereby it was practically interrupted: beginning with the "little horn waxing great toward the pleasant land," and "casting down some of the host" (Da 8:9, 10); namely, when in 171 B.C., or the month Sivan in the year 142 of the era of the Seleucidæ, the sacrifices began to be neglected, owing to the high priest Jason introducing at Jerusalem Grecian customs and amusements, the palæstra and gymnasium; ending with the death of Antiochus, 165 B.C., or the month Shebath, in the year 148 of the Seleucid era. Compare 1 Maccabees 1:11-15; 2 Maccabees 4:9, &c."

Daniel

Study 4 Bible Questions

Daniel 7:9-18

1. Verse 9 – Why is there more than one throne in heaven? How can there be other thrones alongside the throne of the Ancient of Days?

2. Verse 9 – The description of the Ancient of Days is amazing and glorious. How does it compare to the description of Jesus in Revelation 1:12-16? Can we see a family resemblance?

3. Verse 9 – In the description of Jesus in Revelation 1, we learn something about His face. Why doesn't Daniel see the face of the Ancient of Days? Why doesn't anybody ever tell us what His face looks like?

4. Verse 10 – Why is heaven like a court? What are the books that were opened?

5. Verse 11-12 – How can these disturbing verses actually be a great comfort to us in this present age? Who would most appreciate these verses?

6. Verse 13-14 – On the basis of these verses, how would we describe the Son of Man?

7. Verses 13 – What are the 'clouds of heaven'?

8. Verse 18 – If someone asked us how we might become one of these saints who inherits this everlasting kingdom, what would we say?

Study 4 Further Questions

1. Why are the kingdoms depicted as animals? Does each nation have a particular character that can be expressed as an animal? Is this still true today? What animal best depicts your nation?

2. What do you think of when you think of heaven? What do you think it looks like? Do you have any fears or concerns about going there?

3. The Bible is very clear that our final hope is not to go to heaven forever but to live in a renewed physical creation forever and ever. What will happen to heaven after Jesus returns? See Revelation 21.

Study 4 Daily Readings

Day 1	Daniel 7:1-14
Day 2	Daniel 7:15-28
Day 3	Daniel 8:1-27
Day 4	Isaiah 6:1-7
Day 5	Revelation 4:1-11
Day 6	Revelation 5:1-14
Day 7	Ezekiel 1:1-28

The daily Bible readings are an opportunity to not only read through all of the material in the book under study, but also to read parts of the Bible that relate to the themes and issues that we have been considering. We try to make sure that we receive light from the whole Bible as we think through the key issues each week.

Daniel

Study 5 "A Man dressed in linen"

Daniel 9-10

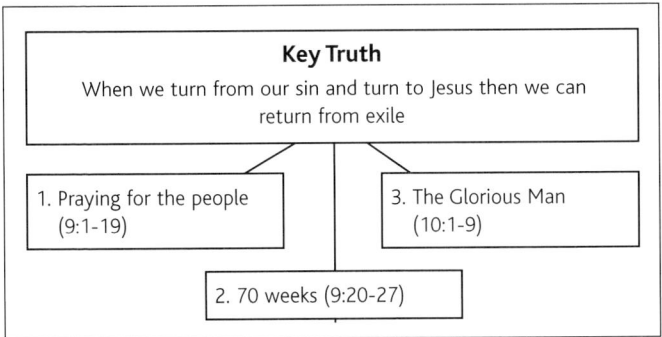

1. Praying for the people (Chapter 9:1-19)

If we can pinpoint the first year of Darius' reign to around 537BC, then it was 69 years after Daniel was taken captive. Daniel had been carefully studying the Bible, especially the prophecies of Jeremiah concerning the length of the exile from Jerusalem.

Jeremiah 29:10 could hardly put the matter more clearly: 'This is what the LORD says: "When seventy years are completed for Babylon, I will come to you and fulfil my gracious promise to bring you back to this place…"'

Thinking that it was nearly time for this prophecy to be fulfiled, Daniel knew how important it was for the lessons of the exile to be learned. He feared that these lessons had not been learned (see verse 13), yet true restoration could only come in the light of true repentance.

He would have remembered what the Law, given nearly 1000 years before, had said about this time. Deuteronomy 30:1-4.

The church might return from exile in a geographical sense, but unless that exile had ended in their hearts and souls then it would mean nothing. While Adam and Eve were still in Eden, the Garden of God, they were already far away from the LORD Jesus (Genesis 3:9-10). Before the exile to Babylon, the people of Israel had enjoyed the temple and all the wonderful presentations of grace and truth through the Law, yet they were far from the LORD God (Isaiah 29:13 – "The Lord says: "These people come near to me with their mouth and honor me with their lips, but their hearts are far from me.").

Daniel was living in exile, far from the Promised Land, without any temple or sacrifices, yet his great concern was that the church return to the LORD God wherever they were living in the world. We can be living in a culture completely opposed to the ways of the Living God and yet we might live and witness in His intimate presence, filled with His Spirit, clothed in His glory. Even now as we still live in this fallen world, still awaiting the Day when the whole creation will end its exile at the return of Jesus, we may yet find our exile ended as we repent, turning from our way of death, turning towards the light and life of Jesus.

Daniel "turned to the Lord God and pleaded with him in prayer and petition, in fasting, and in sackcloth and ashes" (verse 3). It was not enough for Daniel to just think about these things. He had to be humbled, taking off the luxurious clothes of his high position and wearing the most lowly cloth, covering himself in ashes. He took no food, showing that the LORD God was more important to him than bread, that he could live without bread but not without the Word of the LORD – Deut 8:3.

In Genesis 18:27, when Abraham wants to indicate his humble position before the LORD, he describes himself as nothing but 'dust and ashes'. Job sits among the ashes of his ruined possessions and, wearing sackcloth, buries his face in the dust (Job 16:15). Ashes were thrown onto the dump with all the remains of the sacrifices (Leviticus 1:16; 4:12).[66]

Covered in sackcloth and ashes we confess that we are unclean and unworthy. We reject our pride and self-confidence, acknowledging that before the Divine Majesty all that we are, all that we have done, is dirty and worthless. Even the very best we have done amounts to filthy rags (Isaiah 64:6).

---

66 In Numbers 19:17-22 a man made unclean by death must be covered in water and sacrificial ash as part of his cleansing.

Daniel

From such genuine and heartfelt humiliation, we look only to the LORD God to lift us up. If we believe that we can give ourselves a 'good self-image'; if we hope to gain 'self-esteem' from our own therapies and 'self-talk' then will we ever lie in the dust, crying out like Daniel until the LORD God Himself raises us up.

> James 4:8-10 – "Come near to God and he will come near to you. Wash your hands, you sinners, and purify your hearts, you double-minded. Grieve, mourn and wail. Change your laughter to mourning and your joy to gloom. Humble yourselves before the Lord, and he will lift you up."

This is what Daniel did. He not only confesses his sin but also his faith in the Living God. If we think only of our sin we are destroyed by our sin. Yet in the presence of the Most Holy and Gracious God we have the safety to confess all our sins, in all their horror, knowing that His grace is always bigger and stronger than our sin.

Yet, Daniel does so much more than simply confess his own sin. Sometimes we might come across people who think of themselves as 'Christians' without being part of the local church. Such nonsense is so far from Daniel that his prayer takes responsibility for the whole church. Daniel does not think of himself alone but only ever as a part of the church family.

This is surely one of the greatest prayers ever prayed, not only in the Bible but in all history. Throughout this prayer the glorious righteousness of the LORD God and the sinful shame of His people are constantly asserted. Throughout the prayer Daniel states how true and faithful the LORD God is and also how false and unfaithful Israel has been.

We should also remember that such deep and effective prayer comes as a fruit of Daniel's long life of constant daily prayer. In chapter 6 we saw something of the constant and unchangeable patterns of daily prayer that defined the life of Daniel. Daniel knew that he could not possibly maintain a life of faithful service, compassionate love and courageous witness unless he was regularly in genuine fellowship with the Ancient of Days, through the Son of Man, in the power of the Spirit.

The secret of prayer is… prayer. The more time we spend talking to the Living God, then the more we learn how to pray and why it is so important. The Bible is so full of so many encouragements to pray precisely because our sinful, fallen hearts and minds constantly imagine that we can go day after day in our own strength, according to our own wisdom. No matter how often we fall down, no matter how often the same sins defeat us time after time, it is so easy to forget that the answer is simple. If we hide the Word of God in our hearts and regularly pour out our hearts to the Living God only then will we live as Daniel lived, enjoying the gifts and wisdom that he enjoyed.

Verses 4-6: The Lord God has been true to the covenant of love, yet 'we' have never been true to it. Look at all the ways Daniel describes our betrayal: sinned; done wrong; been wicked; rebelled; turned away; not listened. This spiritual adultery from the covenant of love has happened in every generation, from the top to the bottom of the community.

Verses 7-11: The LORD God is righteous, merciful and forgiving, yet we are all covered with shame, wherever we are in the world. Not one of us is free from this condemning shame. Though the Lord mercifully tried to restore us, yet we continually refused to do what He commands in His word.

Verses 12-14: Looking back to the warnings included in the Law nearly a 1000 years before (Deut 28:15-68), Daniel acknowledges that the LORD God has rightly carried out what He threatened.

Verses 15-16: When the Lord has rescued and restored His people when He delivered them from Egypt, He glorified Himself. If His anger is focused on the city of Jerusalem, is there any way for that anger to be turned away?

We must note how Daniel reveals the character of Jesus Christ Himself in this prayer. Daniel takes on himself the sins of the whole nation, from generations long past, as if they were all his own guilt and shame. He stands before the Living God and seeks to turn aside that righteous divine anger against all this wickedness and shameful evil. We will see how Daniel's prayer is answered in verses 20-27 with a very specific promise of the work of Jesus.

Verses 17-19: The Name of the LORD God is the only plea. We have nothing to offer: no righteousness or glory of our own. At the beginning

Daniel

of the prayer all the verbs belonged to us, describing our sin. Here at the end of the prayer all the verbs belong to the LORD God who deals with our sin *for His own sake*: hear our prayers; look with favour; give ear; hear; open your eyes; see; listen; forgive; hear and act; do not delay – "because your city and your people bear your Name" (verse 19).

2. 70 weeks (Chapter 9:20-27)

Even as Daniel was still engaged in this tremendous prayer, the angel Gabriel interrupted him with an answer! Gabriel, we learn, was the man from the earlier vision – 8:15 – who explained the meaning of the Ram and the Goat.

The name 'Gabriel' means 'the mighty one of God'. [67]

Gabriel predicts that a time of seventy sevens will pass after the decree for Jerusalem's restoration is given. [68] That decree was not actually given for before all that Daniel has prayed for will happen – verse 24. Just as Daniel had been so careful and faithful to trust Jeremiah's prophecy of 70 years, now another accurate, time-specific prophecy was given to the church concerning a much greater deliverance: the end of exile for the whole world.

Daniel's great prayer was that the wrath of the Living God be turned away from Jerusalem and that the exile would come to end with a genuine renovation of the heart. The Messiah would come in the seventieth seven and not only atone for sin and bring in everlasting righteousness, but also bring an end to the whole sacrificial system in Jerusalem.

---

[67] In material outside the Bible, Gabriel, Michael, Raphael and Uriel are named as the four most senior created angels (1 Enoch 40:3): the four living creatures who are the closest aides of the Son of Man (see Ezekiel 1:4-18; 10:1-17; Revelation 4:6-8). Only two 'angels' are named in the Bible: Gabriel and Michael ('the one like God'). Some have suggested that Gabriel is none other than the Holy Spirit. Is it possible that Gabriel is the Spirit of God Himself who announces the birth of Jesus to Mary (given that it was His own work to unite Jesus to our humanity)? The work that Gabriel comes to do seems appropriate to the Holy Spirit - "I have now come to give you insight and understanding" (verse 22).

[68] It is also Gabriel who announces the birth of John the Baptist to Zechariah. When Zechariah asks how he can be sure about the miraculous promise, he receives the answer, "I am Gabriel". Presumably this reply was designed to remind Zechariah about the prophecy of Daniel 9, that the seventy 'sevens' was drawing to an end, that the forerunner needed to be born, that the Messiah's birth was at the very door.

> We have here the answer that was immediately sent to Daniel's prayer, and it is a very memorable one, as it contains the most illustrious prediction of Christ and gospel-grace that is extant in all the Old Testament. If John Baptist was the morning-star, this was the day-break to the Sun of righteousness... There were general promises of the coming of the Messiah made to the patriarchs; the preceding prophets had often spoken of him as *one that should come*, but never was the time fixed for his coming until now.[69]

As we have seen in the book of Daniel, things are never quite what they seem. Seventy 'sevens'[70] is not a matter of seventy 'weeks' (a year and 4 months), but 490 years.[71] The 490 years would begin "from the issuing of the decree to restore and rebuild Jerusalem" (verse 23). That decree was not issued for another generation after Daniel, yet when it was issued by King Artaxerxes, recorded for us in book of Ezra, it all happened exactly as Gabriel predicted.

If we consider that the edict for the restoration of Jerusalem was issued by Artaxerxes in 457 BC (see Ezra chapter 4:6-22), then we can see that 490 years after that would put us around 33AD – the very year of Jesus' crucifixion, when atonement was made and everlasting righteousness was established.[72]

The Messiah would accomplish His atoning work in the seventieth week (after first seven 'sevens' and then sixty-two 'sevens – verse 25). "After the sixty-two 'sevens', the Anointed One (the Christ) will be cut off and will have nothing" (verse 26). The seventieth week of Daniel's vision covers the time of Jesus public ministry, atoning death, resurrection and ascension.

---

69 Matthew Henry on Daniel chapter 9.

70 If the number seven is the number of completion in the Bible, then surely the event that is the completion of all things must come at the end of 70 sets of 7!

71 The 490 years is divided up into sections: seven 'sevens' - 49 years; sixty two 'sevens' - 434 years; one 'seven' - 7 years. Various scholars have suggested a wide variety of explanations of how these three divisions correspond to specific historical events. For example, Matthew Henry - "Concerning the division of them into seven weeks, and sixty-two weeks, and one week; and the reason of this is as hard to account for as any thing else. In the first seven weeks, or forty-nine years, the temple and city were built; and in the last single week Christ preached his gospel, by which the Jewish economy was taken down..."

72 Furthermore, Gabriel came at the time of the evening sacrifice (verse 21). Many saints believe that it was at the very hour when Jesus died at the time of the evening sacrifice.

Daniel

However, a terrible warning is also given (verses 26-27). The destruction that had come on Jerusalem at the time of the exile 70 years before, would happen again after the Messiah's atonement. In Daniel chapter 8 warning was given of a hard time during the time of the Greeks (8:9-12, 23-25), but that would be eclipsed by an even worse calamity that would destroy Jerusalem and the temple. The Messiah's work would mean that there would be no longer any need for sacrifice and offering at the temple, but the destruction from this 'ruler' will make such things impossible. He will set up "an abomination that causes desolation" (verse 27).

Jesus Himself stated that this prophecy of Daniel 9:26-27 was about to be fulfiled after His own death and resurrection, Matthew 24:15-16

> …when you see standing in the holy place 'the abomination that causes desolation,' spoken of through the prophet Daniel – let the reader understand – then let those who are in Judea flee to the mountains…

If Daniel's concern was for the temple and Jerusalem, all these prophecies may well have left him "exhausted and ill for several days" (8:27). He has learned that during the time of the Greek empire, terrible sacrilege will happen in the temple, bringing a temporary end to the sacrifices. He has also learned that although the Messiah will make atonement 490 years after the decree the rebuilding of Jerusalem, yet after that Jerusalem and the temple will be completely destroyed and no sacrifices or offerings will be made there again.

If Daniel's hope was fixed on Jerusalem and the temple then he could see only a bleak future. However, if Daniel's hope was fixed on Jesus, the long Promised Messiah, the Divine Son of Man, then these prophecies must have filled him with joy unspeakable and full of glory. If he was one of the prophets who searched with the greatest care for the time and circumstances of the sufferings and glory of the Messiah, then this would have been a day of great rejoicing and worship.

3. The Glorious Man (Chapter 10:1-9)

Now more than 80 years old, Daniel was still full of zeal for the Living God. He set himself to prayer and fasting, rejecting all choice food or wine and denying himself all luxuries. Since his youth Daniel had exercised this self-control in the Name of the LORD God and after more than 65 years of such discipline he was still hungry and thirsty for the Bread of Life and the streams of Living Water.

This time of fasting happened during the time of Passover and Unleavened Bread – verse 4. These first festivals of the Levitical year (see Leviticus 23) were designed to bring a deep awareness of the desperate need for the atonement that the Messiah would bring. As Daniel remembered how the Angel of the LORD brought judgement on the mighty nation of Egypt and the Egyptian 'gods', perhaps Daniel wondered when this would happen to all the nations. When would the great final exodus happen, when the whole world would be turned into the everlasting Promised Land as the family home of the Living God?

After three weeks of humbling himself before the Living God he receives a personal visit from the Son of Man. Why was Daniel in this time of 'mourning' – verse 2? Some wonder if it was the reluctance of many of the exiles to return to the rebuilding work of Jerusalem and the temple. Perhaps the vision of the seventy 'sevens' filled him with such concern for the unfolding of history, the meaning of history, that he needed to know more. Who could unroll the scroll of history? Who could unlock the meaning of all the turmoil and conflict in the world? How would history come to its conclusion? What would be the final outcome of all things?

Daniel was standing by the river Tigris with other people – verse 4 & 7. The river Tigris is one of the four great rivers that flowed out from the Garden of Eden – Genesis 2:14 – and although that great river source is long removed from our realm, we can well understand why Daniel might love to stand by this fallen shadow of the original Tigris.

When Daniel looked up he was confronted with an overwhelming vision of the glorious Son of Man, the pre-incarnate Jesus in His great glory.

Daniel

We can have no doubt as to the identity of this Glorious Man when we compare His description with the description provided by the apostle John in Revelation 1:12-17.

Notice that John refers to Jesus as someone 'like a son of man', deliberately reminding us of the prophecy of Daniel – Rev 1:13. Just as John fell to the ground as though dead in the presence of Jesus, so Daniel reacts in the same way – verse 9. When the apostle Paul was granted such a visitation from Jesus on his way to Damascus, the men around him saw nothing but were overwhelmed with terror (Acts 9:1-9). In the same way the men with Daniel did not see the vision of Jesus but ran away in terror to hide.

> …The Son of God, the Messiah; who, though not as yet incarnate, yet was so in the counsel and purpose of God; had agreed in covenant to be man, was promised and prophesied as such; and now appeared in human form, as he frequently did before the incarnation, as a pledge of it, and showing his readiness to assume human nature: he appears here 'clothed in linen', in the habit of a priest; which office he sustains and executes by sacrifice of himself and by his prevalent intercession…[73]

These priestly robes of the Divine Man are so important for us to meditate on. Leviticus 16:4 indicates that even the human copies of this Great High Priest also wore linen robes. As Daniel was filled with the thoughts of Passover, how vital it was for him to be reminded of this Divine High Priest who doesn't minister at the ruined temple of Jerusalem but at the heavenly reality. To know that the Living God is His own High Priest is the greatest comfort in life and death.

Daniel knew that the one Living God is the Ancient of Days, the Son of Man and the Divine Spirit – yet here he sees the Son of Man clothed in His high priestly garments. To know that the Divine Son of Man who has such open access to the Ancient of Days is the Mediator, the Priest who makes atonement for the world… this is the most precious of all truths. Hebrews 8:3-6.

---

73 John Gill in his commentary on Daniel 10:5

We might compare Daniel's description of Jesus with John's description.

Daniel's description of Jesus	John's description of Jesus
Dressed in linen	Dressed in a robe
Belt of finest gold	Golden sash around the chest
Body like chrysolite or beryl [74]	Head and hair like snow
Face like lightning	Face like the sun in its brilliance
Eyes like flaming torches	Eyes like blazing fire
Arms like polished bronze	In His hand were seven stars
Legs like polished bronze	Feet like bronze in a furnace
Voice like the sound of a multitude	Voice like the sound of rushing waters

Although John does not mention the body of Jesus, yet he has more to say of His head. Notice also that for Daniel the feet and legs of Jesus were of polished bronze whereas John sees that they have been in the furnace.[75]

Confronted with the utterly glorious and wonderful LORD God of Abraham, Isaac and Jacob, the Alpha and Omega, the Son of Man, the Divine Messiah, the Angel of the LORD… Daniel is stripped of all earthly strength – verses 7-9. As soon as the LORD Jesus began to speak to him he collapsed to the ground as if he were dead.

Jesus is the visible form of the invisible God and many people throughout the Scriptures have seen His appearance. However, simply because it is possible for Him to be seen yet it is always an incomprehensible miracle, an incredible marvel of gracious power and mercy. His glory must always be heavily veiled in all His dealings with this exiled world. In His incarnation He had to entirely lay aside that uncreated glory and only at the Transfiguration did He briefly allow a tiny flicker of that majesty to shine out. To the exhausted Elijah, the Angel of the LORD comes in such

---

[74] The Biblical word may refer to either chrysolite or beryl. Both are aluminium silicates. They may be translucent and can be different colours, including golden or green or blue. When we consider Ezekiel's description in Ezekiel 1:27 we might conclude that the body of the glorious Lord Jesus has a glowing golden appearance.

[75] Many of the saints down the centuries have noticed this difference, concluding that Jesus had not yet been through the furnace of the Cross when Daniel saw Him.

Daniel

gentleness with His glory set aside – 1 Kings 19:1-9. To 80-year-old Moses at the burning bush, more of His divine majesty is revealed. Isaiah sees just the hem of the Divine priestly robes and is completely shattered by the experience.

Daniel is granted a vision of Jesus – and from this vision Daniel was able to gaze out across all the chaos and rebellion of human history with the joy and peace that comes from seeing the Alpha and the Omega, the Beginning and the End.

Study 5 Bible Questions

Daniel 9:4-19

1. Verse 4 – Why does Daniel begin with such a high view of the LORD God? If he feels so bad about his sin, doesn't that simply make it all seem worse?

2. Verse 4 – The covenant is the plan of salvation, the gospel set out by the Trinity from before the world began. How does Daniel describe the covenant?

3. Verses 5-6 – List all the verbs that are used to describe the way we have betrayed our loving LORD. Which ones speak to us most?

4. Verses 7-11 – Why does Daniel list all the sins of earlier generations? Why take responsibility for things he didn't even do?

5. Verses 11b-14 – In the Law, why did the LORD God describe the consequences of rejecting His law in such detail? Why spend more time on the curses rather than the blessings? See Deuteronomy 28:15-68.

6. Verses 15-19 – What is the basis of Daniel's prayer for mercy?

7. What lessons can we learn for our own prayer life? Spend some time now praying a Daniel 9 prayer of repentance. How can we repent for the weakness, the lack of practical love and the betrayal of living truth in recent generations?

Daniel

Study 5 Further Questions

1. What is the value of present day governments apologising for wrongs done by earlier generations? Do these words of apology need to be backed up with practical compensation or other changes in behaviour?

2. If the Bible is so filled with amazingly detailed and accurate predictions, should we use them more in our explanations of the gospel? Should we only speak of the predictions of Jesus or can we even show how Antiochus Epiphanes was prophesied? Are there any dangers in that?

3. Should we ever pray to be given the sort of vision of Christ that Daniel received in chapter 10, even though it nearly killed him. Why doesn't Jesus give these visions all the time?

Study 5 Daily Readings

Day 1	Daniel 9:1-14
Day 2	Deuteronomy 28:1-14
Day 3	Deuteronomy 28:15-44
Day 4	Deuteronomy 28:45-68
Day 5	Daniel 9:15-27
Day 6	1 Corinthians 10:1-13
Day 7	Daniel 10:1-11:1

The daily Bible readings are an opportunity to not only read through all of the material in the book under study, but also to read parts of the Bible that relate to the themes and issues that we have been considering. We try to make sure that we receive light from the whole Bible as we think through the key issues each week.

King of the Beasts

Daniel

Study 6 "The Great Prince who protects your people"

Daniel 10:10-12:13

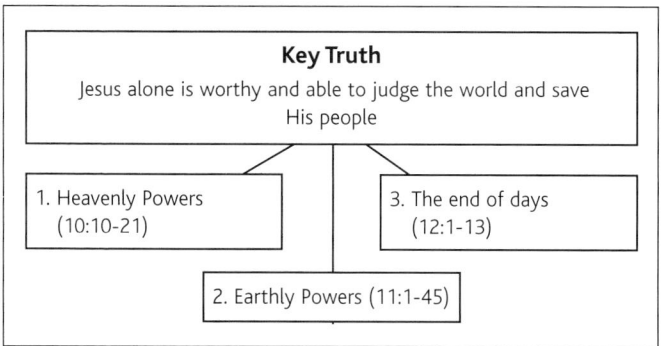

1. Heavenly Powers (Chapter 10:10-21)

Daniel was granted a vision of Jesus that was almost too much for his physical frame. It was so vital for Daniel to see more of this glorious Son of Man who is one with the Ancient of Days. In the confusion of the nations, in the conflicts and arrogant wars of the four beasts or the collisions between the ram and the goat, yet so much greater than all these petty events of world history is One so wonderful, so glorious, so majestic that He alone is worthy to unlock the history of the universe.

Jesus alone is the Rock on which all history is built. To see Him is to see the meaning of history, the end and the beginning all in Him.

Daniel chapter 10 is the key to all the wars and rumours of wars in Daniel chapter 11. Human empires and kingdoms come and go. The world is full of wars and rumours of wars – and so it will be to the end of the age. The human principalities and powers imagine that they are the masters of their own realms and dominions, yet above them the principalities and powers of the heavenly realms also wrestle with each other for power and influence. Yet, even they are all also finally completely controlled and determined by the Great, Divine Prince – the Son of Man who has all authority in heaven and on earth.

The Son of Man	Jesus the King of all Kings, the Divine High Priest, the Angel of the LORD	Daniel 2:20-23; 4:1-3, 34-35; 6:26-27; 7:9-14; 10:5-9; 12:1-4
The Heavenly Princes and Powers	The Prince of Persia & The Prince of Greece… and The Princes of Babylon, Rome, Britain, India, America, China etc.	Daniel 7:1-7; 8:1-27; 10:12-14, 20-11:1
The Earthly Princes and Powers	Nebuchadnezzar, Darius, Cyrus, Alexander, Antiochus Epiphanes, Nero etc. etc.	Daniel 1:1-2, 21; 2:1; 3:1; 4:1; 5:1, 30; 6:1; 7:1; 8:1; 9:1; 10:1

Daniel was serving as a senior civil servant in the ancient empire of Babylon and then Persia. Both of these Gentile nations were dedicated to the aims and goals of the nations of this world, yet Daniel earned great respect for the exceptional way he pursued this career. Being one of the best citizens that these empires ever knew was in no opposition to being a true citizen of the Heavenly Kingdom of the Living God. We are in the world without being part of the world. We submit to the authorities that the LORD God has appointed out of reverence for Christ.

To see how the LORD Jesus is the glorious King above all the kings and powers of this passing age was so important for Daniel… as it is for us all. If we are to serve faithfully in whatever career we pursue we must both work with diligence as if we were working for Jesus and also work with a true perspective, aware that our careers in this age are not of ultimate importance. It is all too easy to allow our identity and our values become enmeshed with our nationality, our career, our status, our money, and our possessions. Only as we keep the glorious vision of Jesus at the front of our hearts and minds can we see with clarity and act with wisdom. The nations of the world will one day all become the Kingdom of our God – Revelation 11:15. If we can work for His Kingdom while submitting to these passing kingdoms we can bear witness to His glory even in the chaos of the beasts emerging from the sea (Daniel chapter 7).

Can we see the ebb and flow of the nations and empires and economies of the world all around the fixed Rock of Jesus?

Can we see that the real issues of history are determined in the courts of heaven?

Daniel

Can we see that the empires and nations of the world are in a deep sense controlled by principalities and powers, not only from this world but also from the heavenly realms?

Struck down by the vision of Jesus, Daniel was assisted to get onto his hands and knees – Daniel 10:10. To whom does this hand belong that touches Daniel? Could it be one of the created angels who assist the Son of Man? Was it one of the mighty living creatures, the Watchers filled with eyes? Could it even be Gabriel?[76]

> Not the hand of the Man clothed with linen, whose voice he heard and whose hand was like polished brass (Dan 10:6), but the hand of one distinct from Him, one of His attendants (Dan 12:5) that had the similitude of the sons of men (Dan 10:16) and whose hand was softer and nearer a human one; very probably the hand of the Angel Gabriel in human form, who had touched him before, when in like circumstances (Dan 8:16).[77]

The words of reassurance given to Daniel help him to stand up. Ever since Daniel began to pray he had been heard in the courts of heaven – verse 12. This angel had been sent to give Daniel a deeper understanding of "what will happen to your people in the future" (verse 14). It is vital to remember the purpose of the message of Daniel chapter 11. It is NOT to give a general prediction of middle eastern history for the next few hundred years, but to give an understanding of what kind of future the church was going to face.

The angel had been delayed in some kind of conflict with the "prince of the Persian kingdom". Some understand this to mean that the angel had been trying to influence or thwart or direct the affairs of Cyrus, the king of Persia mentioned in 10:1. However, it is important to note that whereas Cyrus is called the "king" of Persia, this adversary is called the "prince' of Persia.

---

76 If Gabriel were the Holy Spirit it would help us to understand why Daniel speaks to 'my Lord' and the character of the speech in verse 18 when Daniel is granted peace and strength. However, it is hard to see how the Prince of Persia would be able to detain the Holy Spirit for 21 days!

77 John Gill's commentary. Matthew Henry takes a similar view - "It should seem, it was not he whose glory he saw in vision (v. 5, 6) that here touched him, and talked with him; that was Christ, but this seems to have been the angel Gabriel, whom Christ had once before ordered to instruct Daniel, ch. viii. 16".

The same kind of language occurs in Ezekiel 28 and Isaiah 14. In Ezekiel 28:1-10 the 'ruler of Tyre' is told, "you are a man and not a god" even though he liked to think of himself as a god. Yet, in Ezekiel 28:11-19 the 'king of Tyre' is addressed as someone who had been in the Garden of Eden, a guardian cherub (verse 14), one who was expelled from the mountain of God. It is easy to see that both the human ruler of Tyre and Satan himself are addressed in this condemnation of Tyre.[78] We see the same pattern in Isaiah 13-14 when the 'king of Babylon' is called Lucifer, the morning star who was fallen from heaven.

In this same way we can see that Satan and his angels stand behind the thrones and powers of the kingdoms of this passing age, trying to determine the character and direction of the nations of the world. These heavenly powers work to control the earthly powers.

In a deep sense, our study of human history can only ever look at one aspect of the stage, one set of the actors in the play. On the other side of the stage there is another cast acting in the heavenly realm. We look for cause and effects in history, and after the dust has settled we point to whatever economic, social or political factors that seem to explain all that has happened. Yet, beyond our sight, beyond our study, beyond our control, powers and influences are at work known only to the courts of heaven, to the Son of Man and His Heavenly host.

Paul's words in Ephesians 6:10-12 are so profound: "Be strong in the Lord and in his mighty power. Put on the full armour of God so that you can take your stand against the devil's schemes. For our struggle is not against flesh and blood, but against the rulers, against the authorities, against the powers of this dark world and against the spiritual forces of evil in the heavenly realms."

Notice that Paul sees the ultimate adversary as the devil, with his evil schemes. Those schemes are presented to us on two levels: first, the political powers of this dark world in the earthly realm; second, the

---

78 It is interesting to note that the Baal worshipping culture of Tyre and Sidon was transplanted to North Africa to form the Carthaginian Empire, at the heart of which was the temple to Baal in Carthage, characterised by the sacrifice of infants in the fire.

spiritual forces of evil in the heavenly realms. The powers of this dark world are obviously connected to the forces of evil in heavenly realms, woven together in the devil's schemes.

Against such a complex and mighty army of adversaries, spanning the world and history, how can we possibly stand? How can we hope to wrestle against such forces?

In the rest of Ephesians 6 Paul explains that far from trying to directly engage with these spiritual powers, our job is to hold firm to the gospel of Jesus: holding firm to the truth, righteousness, peace, faith and salvation which the Holy Spirit gives us in Jesus. Only as we faithfully and courageously persist in obeying the teaching of Jesus, following His Way, can we stand firm and conquer in His Name. We cannot tackle the prince of Persia, Greece or any other regional principality, yet what we can do is put the Way of Jesus into practice in our families, communities and nations. The powers of this dark world (the structures, institutions, attitudes and systems) may have been directed away from Jesus by the devil's schemes, but the wonder is that as the followers of Jesus consistently live as He lived then the revolution of His kingdom is felt in communities and even nations.[79]

Notice that both Daniel and Paul in Ephesians 6:18 regard *prayer* as the key to all this. Daniel and his companions faced the dark powers against them whether through the statue of chapter 3, Belshazzar's decadent culture of chapter 5 or the prayer ban in chapter 6. We see Daniel's consistent life of prayer and therefore his consistent life of faithful witness, standing firm in the strength of the LORD.

The angel was detained in strife with the prince of Persia, but victory was instant and complete when the mighty Michael entered the scene – verse 13. Michael means 'the One like God' and many draw conclusions about the identity of this One like God.

---

[79] I will never forget how a group of Christians put so much time into trying to bind the spiritual powers of poverty in an area of London when what we all really needed to do was simply help people in poverty with very practical assistance. As James says, the sign of real religion is to give real concrete help to those in need – James 1:27; 2:14-17.

> Here is Michael our prince, the great protector of the church, and the patron of its just but injured cause: The first of the chief princes, v. 13. Some understand it of a created angel, but an archangel of the highest order... Others think that Michael the archangel is no other than Christ himself, the angel of the covenant, and the Lord of the angels, he whom Daniel saw in vision, v. 5. He came to help me (v. 13); and there is none but he that holds with me in these things, v. 21. Christ is the church's prince; angels are not, Heb. ii. 5. He presides in the affairs of the church and effectually provides for its good.[80]

The Geneva Bible with classic simplicity explains: "Even though God could by one angel destroy all the world, yet to assure His children of His love He sends forth double power, even Michael, that is, Christ Jesus the head of angels."

The heavenly powers might try to take charge of the nations, but the Son of Man, Jesus Christ, takes charge of His church. As we follow Him and abide in Him, we need have no concern about the devil's schemes or the dark powers of this world or the spiritual forces in the heavenly realms. They are not able to resist Him for even one moment!

Daniel was so physically shattered by the vision of Jesus, as an 85-year-old man, that he needed special strengthening to continue – verses 15-19. Just as Isaiah needed special angelic assistance in Isaiah 6:6-7, so Daniel receives the message that is so often given by the LORD God to His people – "Do not be afraid. Be at peace. Be strong."[81]

Faced with a world in conflict and a church heading towards constant persecution, it is no surprise that we might feel weak or afraid. Yet, if we trust that even in the darkness and turmoil, the LORD Jesus will never let us go and never forsake us, then the fear falls away and His strength renews us.

---

80 Matthew Henry

81 Compare Genesis 15:1; 21:17; see Moses words in Exodus 14:13; or Joshua's words in Numbers 14:9; Deut 31:6; Joshua 8:1 and then Joshua's words in Joshua 10:25; Judges 6:23; Isaiah 40:9; 41:14; Matthew 1:20; 28:5, 10; Acts 18:9; 27:24; Rev 1:17

Daniel

The angel informs Daniel that after battling with the prince of Persia he must go onto conflict with the prince of Greece – verse 20. This is to be expected given the visions of chapter 7 and 8, but before these events unfold he is allowed to inform Daniel what is written in the Book of Truth.

It is so wonderfully reassuring to know that the history of the world has already been written and it is all in the Book of Truth. The chapters have already been determined and the outcome has been appointed. The final chapter is already there to be read – and we will see something of that final chapter in Daniel chapter 12.

The dark powers of this world may feel that the future can be anything they want it to be[82] and the spiritual forces of the heavenly realms may have no end of schemes and alliances, yet all that they do is already written, appointed by the holy covenant of the Living God.

Even today as we look at various empires and ideologies that seem to threaten the world and the church, we can live and die for the Kingdom of Jesus in the peace and strength that come from knowing that the Son of Man reigns and that He has already written the Book of Truth.

2. Earthly Powers (Chapter 11:1-45)

The key to understanding all that is going on in this chapter is given back in Daniel chapter 2:20-21

> Daniel praised the God of heaven and said: "Praise be to the name of God for ever and ever; wisdom and power are his. He changes times and seasons; he sets up kings and deposes them.

Throughout the chapter, when it seems that the book of history is written by the King of the North and the King of the South we are constantly reminded of "the appointed time" and "the holy covenant". No matter what they do, no matter what alliances they make or armies they raise, yet their destiny is appointed by the Son of Man through His holy covenant.

Notice also that the King of the North and the King of the South are spoken of as individuals who last for many generations of human history.

---

82 Many empires have tried to destroy the church of the Living God – and all have failed. The church is still here, growing across the world each day, yet all these empires have disappeared.

We seem to be reminded that behind the human kings and generals, nations and kingdoms, there are principalities and powers in the heavenly realms who shape them all.

We do not have the time or space to attempt a detailed chart mapping each prediction of Daniel chapter 11 onto precise historical events, and scholars disagree about many of these details. However, the purpose of the chapter is not to provide an advance history lesson but to prepare the church for the challenges and persecutions that she will face in all history. The church lived on from Daniel's day right down to the ministry of Jesus in the seventieth 'seven' predicted in chapter 7, surrounded by wars and rumours of wars, subject to times of severe persecution and trouble. Yet, just as Daniel chapter 11 had predicted, all that had been appointed came to pass and the holy covenant of the LORD God was fulfiled just as it was written.

This is the key lesson for the church in every age. Jesus warned us that we would be constantly surrounded by wars and rumours of wars until that final day when He returns on the Day of Divine Justice. There will be earthquakes, famines, false-Christs and even times of almost unbearable deception and persecution. Yet, through it all we are to stand firm, looking only to that Glorious Son of Man who is able to deliver us from everything. Whether we live or die in these times of trouble, yet we are utterly safe in the hands of the Jesus who will call us back to life in His everlasting kingdom – see Daniel 12:2.

Consider how Jesus Himself explained the teaching of Daniel chapter 11. With brilliant simplicity and matchless clarity, the Master Bible scholar sets out the key truth of this excerpt from the Book of truth – Matthew 24:6-13.

The end of the world will come but not before long periods of war, conflict and disaster. When these things happen it is so easy to imagine that it is the end of the world. NO! It may be the end of our world, our life, yet we need to keep our nerve and continue to love with warmth, standing firm in Jesus, bearing witness to His truth and kingdom in the whole world.

It may be worth noting the historical details of the very first predictions of Daniel 11 so that we can see the extraordinary accuracy of all that the angel revealed from the Book of Truth.

Daniel

Verse	Description	Historical event
2	Three kings and then a richer fourth king Cambyses	(529-523 BC); Pseudo-Smerdis (523-522 BC); Darius Hystapes (522-485 BC); Xerxes (486-465 BC)
3	Mighty king	Alexander the Great (-301 BC)
4	Divided kingdom	Ptolemy of Egypt; Seleucus of Syria; Antigonus; Cassander
5	King of the South	Egypt under the Ptolemaic dynasty
6	King of the North	Persia under the Seleucid dynasty

The divided Greek empire entered a long period of conflict between the Seleucid's of Persia (the King of the North) and the Ptolemy's of Egypt (the King of the South), with the land of Israel caught between this warring kingdoms.[83] Torn between the two powers of this dark world, the church had hundreds of years of trouble ahead, leading up to the terrible events of the reign of Antiochus described in verses 21-45. Just as in the gospels, so here, Jesus warns His church to expect opposition and persecution in this passing age.

Daniel receives such a lot of detail about this time of extreme persecution because there would be no more canonical prophets of God left at that time to sustain and direct the church.

> All this is a prophecy of the reign of Antiochus Epiphanes, the little horn spoken of before (chapter 8:9) a sworn enemy to the Jewish religion, and a bitter persecutor of those that adhered to it. What troubles the Jews met with in the reigns of the Persian kings were not so particularly foretold to Daniel as these, because then they had living prophets with them, Haggai and Zechariah, to encourage

---

[83] It may be worth remembering how the points of the compass function within the Scriptures. The sun rises in the east and sets in the west, charting the way back from exile to the presence of the Living God who dwells in unapproachable light. If the gospel direction is from east to west, then what of north and south? It has been suggested that the north and the south simply describe all the nations of the world - (Psalm 89:12). If this is so, then Daniel chapter 11 is not only telling us about the kingdoms of Syria and Egypt but setting a general pattern for the constant wars and conflicts that are true of the world in every age, in every region.

them; but these troubles in the days of Antiochus were foretold, because, before that time, prophecy would cease, and they would find it necessary to have recourse to the written word... Of the kings that came after Antiochus nothing is here prophesied, for that was the most malicious mischievous enemy to the church, that was a type of the son of perdition, whom the Lord shall consume with the breath of his mouth and destroy with the brightness of his coming, and none shall help him. (Matthew Henry)

The Scriptures do seem to indicate that there may well be another time of persecution for the church like that dreadful time under Antiochus (see 2 Thess 2:1-11). At that time, and whenever we face such severe opposition from the kingdoms of this dark world, we need to return to these Scriptures. However much history may seem to be out of control, yet the path of suffering is also the path of glory in fellowship with the Son of Man. If we fear the One who has all power over our eternal destiny then we need have no fear of those who can do nothing more than kill our bodies – Matthew 10:28.

3. The end of days (Chapter 12:1-13)

Chapter 11 has shown us the church of the Living God surrounded by hostile kingdoms that pursue their selfish dreams with no concern for the holy covenant of the LORD God. What hope do we have? Where can we find refuge and strength in these times of trouble?

Looking ahead, perhaps to an unprecedented time of suffering at the end of all history (verse 1), yet Daniel is shown not hopelessness but the glorious certain hope of deliverance from Michael, "the great prince who protects your people".

The Geneva Bible has an excellent little summary of what we read here: "The angel here notes two things: first that the Church will be in great affliction and trouble at Christ's coming, and next that God will send His Angel to deliver it, whom he here calls Michael, meaning Christ, who is proclaimed by the preaching of the gospel."

The great, final deliverance that the LORD Jesus will bring will be the final and total triumph of good over evil, the day of justice when all wrongs are put right and the defeat of death itself.

Daniel

> ...at that time your people – everyone whose name is found written in the book – will be delivered. Multitudes who sleep in the dust of the earth will awake: some to everlasting life, others to shame and everlasting contempt. Those who are wise will shine like the brightness of the heavens, and those who lead many to righteousness, like the stars forever and ever.

On the Day of Jesus there will be an incredible general resurrection when everybody who has ever lived, whether good or evil, will be called back to physical life in order to be judged.

What a day! The evil that seemed to go unpunished, that seemed to be forgotten in the mists of time, will be brought to justice. The crimes that the police never solved will all be laid bare. The thoughts and fantasies that seemed to be locked secure in our hearts and minds will all be brought out into the clear light of day for all to see. Every careless word we have spoken will be accounted for and judged – Matthew 12:36. For those who face the Divine Judge in their own strength it will bring "shame and everlasting contempt".

Yet for those of us who have found refuge in Jesus, it will be a day of such glory and rejoicing. Whatever shame and contempt, suffering and death, we faced in this dark world of conflict will be utterly swallowed up in the everlasting resurrection life of Jesus. From being the despised and ignored we will then "shine like the brightness of the heavens" forever and ever.

Note how the greatest glory of that day will be reserved for those who have spent their lives leading many to righteousness – verse 3. The dark forces of this world, the flesh and the devil will always try to persuade us not to bother sharing the gospel of Jesus with others. We will hear no end of reasons why we should ignore everybody else and yet those with the loving heart and faithful courage of Jesus will, on that day, be shown to shine like the brightest of stars. If now we might feel despised for bearing witness to Jesus, on that day we will be the stars of the show!

> The more good any do in this world, especially to the souls of men, the greater will be their glory and reward in the other world. Those that turn men to righteousness, that turn sinners from the errors of their ways and help to save their souls from death (Jam. v. 20), will share in the glory of those they have helped to heaven, which will be a great addition to their own glory. (Matthew Henry)

It has been said that the ancient church of the Old Testament did not really have a clear understanding of our resurrection future! Surely all such empty ideas are destroyed by the glorious words of this final section of Daniel's book.

Daniel had recorded a lot of information since the vision of Jesus at the beginning of chapter 10, yet he was to seal it up so that it would be appreciated at the proper time – verse 4. Can we imagine the alarm and confusion that this prophecy could have caused in his day in the minds of those without proper wisdom and balance? Even today when the detailed events of Daniel chapter 11 are long gone, all kinds of people obsess about the details and become lost in mazes of speculation.

Daniel had to make this book secure, possibly giving it to trusted and wise saints who would be able to bring it out in the time of Antiochus when many people would be desperately looking for insight and knowledge – verse 4.[84]

Daniel himself, one of the wisest and deepest saints in the Bible (see Ezekiel 28:3), is perplexed by this vision – verse 8. He has heard so many things predicted stretching away to the very end of the world. When was all this going to happen? How long would it all take? What was the date of that glorious day of resurrection? (This is a common question that saints of every age are tempted to obsess about!)

Jesus Christ remained above the waters of the Tigris, with one angel on each of the river banks – verses 5-7. When one of the angels enquired as the timescale of all these things, He gave that symbolic reply that we considered back in chapter 7. Just as the time of the fourth beast's persecution of the church was described as three and a half years in 7:25, so here in chapter 12 the LORD Jesus says that all this long history of the church in a world of conflict and opposition will be just three and a half years.

It sounds a lot longer than three and a half years! In human history it would last for hundreds of years till the birth of Jesus, and since then more than 2,000 years. Yet, in this symbolism of the Bible it is all just

---

84 In Revelation 22:10-11 an angel gives the opposite advice to John. John's prophecy was not for some future generations, but was needed right then and there, and in every age of the church ever since.

Daniel

"three and a half years". This time of suffering and opposition is only for 'three and a half years' – half of the complete time (a 'week' of time).

Our job is not to waste our time trying to date the end of the world, a date that even Jesus was not concerned about – Matthew 24:36. These troubles will soon be over and then the resurrection future will dawn. See Romans 8:17-21 and 2 Corinthians 4:17.

Daniel's only question concerns this final outcome.

How will history end?

What is the final chapter of that marvellous Book of Truth? (Daniel 10:21)

Daniel is told that such knowledge is too great even for him – verse 9. What we will be like in that resurrection future is beyond what we can now imagine. Remember what the apostle John said concerning that final chapter – 1 John 3:1-3.

The saints who have this hope will have the wisdom to wait patiently for the end, holding firm to the Way, Truth and Life of Jesus. The wicked will continue to pursue their foolish and wicked ways whether they read the words of prophecy or not.

Verses 11-12 might initially seem very strange until we remember the symbolic meaning of the three and half years (1290 days).[85] The time may seem long and yet it will not be long. Even if it seems to go on even longer than expected (the extra 45 days added in verse 12), yet the end will certainly come and everyone who faithfully, patiently waits will be blessed.[86]

---

85 The Geneva Bible comments on the 1290 days saying "signifying that the time will be long until Christ's second coming, and yet the children of God ought not to be discouraged, even though it is deferred." However, many take this to be a literal description of the length of time that Antiochus Epiphanes was in control of Jerusalem – during which time he ended the daily sacrifice and committed the abomination that causes desolation when he offered pig sacrifices to Zeus in the temple. Josephus, the great Jewish historian of the first century AD, claimed that this period lasted for three and a half years.

86 Richard Bewes makes a very helpful suggestion. "Perhaps the answer is that, back in Daniel's time, the HEBREW calendar was based on lunar, not solar, months. The lunar year – based on the moon – was eleven days less than the solar year, based on the sun. So periodically they had to insert an extra thirteenth month; in fact it seems that they sometimes had to insert an extra twelfth month, AND an extra sixth month, within the lunar cycle. So there's no need to assume an inconsistency with these figures."

We have seen the deep parallels between the book of Daniel and the book of Revelation as we have gone through these studies. It may well be useful to note how Daniel 12:12 is echoed time and time again in the book of Revelation in the final words of each of the seven letters in Revelations chapter 2 & 3. We must endure to the end, through all the trials, and then we will receive all the wonderful blessings that Jesus is bringing with Him.

Daniel was an old man with a long life of faithful hard work behind him. It was almost time for him to leave this life and go to be with Jesus confident of a glorious resurrection future – verse 13.

We give the final word to our faithful friend Matthew Henry who applies that final verse of the book of Daniel with such a loving pastor's heart.

> Daniel was now very old, and had been long engaged both in an intimate acquaintance with heaven and in a great deal of public business on this earth. And now he must think of bidding farewell to this present state: 'Go thou thy way till the end be'.
>
> (1.) It is good for us all to think much of going away from this world; we are still going, and must be gone shortly, gone the way of all the earth. That must be our way; but this is our comfort, We shall not go till God calls for us to another world, and till he has done with us in this world…
>
> (2.) When a good man goes his way from this world he enters into rest…
>
> (3.) Time and days will have an end; not only our time and days will end very shortly, but all times and days will have an end at length; yet a little while, and time shall be no more, but all its revolutions will be numbered and finished.
>
> (4.) Our rest in the grave will be but till the end of the days; and then the peaceful rest will be happily disturbed by a joyful resurrection.
>
> (5.) We must every one of us stand in our lot at the end of the days. In the judgment of the great day we must have our allotment according to what we were, and what we did, in the body, either,

Come, you blessed or, Go, you cursed; and we must stand for ever in that lot. It was a comfort to Daniel, it is a comfort to all the saints, that, whatever their lot is in the days of time, they shall have a happy lot in the end of the days, shall have their lot among the chosen. And it ought to be the great care and concern of every one of us to secure a happy lot at last in the end of the days, and then we may well be content with our present lot, welcome the will of God.

(6.) A believing hope and prospect of a blessed lot in the heavenly Canaan, at the end of the days, will be an effectual support to us when we are going our way out of this world, and will furnish us with living comforts in dying moments.

Study 6   Bible Questions

Daniel 12:1-13

1. Verse 1 – Don't spend too long on this question, but do we feel convinced that Michael is Christ? What are the arguments for and against?

2. Verse 1 – Throughout the book of Daniel the church is warned that terrible persecution lies ahead. Jesus tells His followers the same thing – Luke 21:12; John 15:20. Paul repeats this teaching in general – 2 Timothy 3:12 – and in particular concerning a time of unprecedented persecution – 2 Thessalonians 2:1-12. The book of Revelation also seems to indicate severe persecution before Jesus returns. Why do we need to know this?

3. Verses 1-2 – From dust we came and to dust we return… until that final day of resurrection. Why is *everybody* resurrected, whether good or evil – whether for life or for shame?

4. Verse 3 – The followers of Jesus will be like the bright heavens and the stars forever and ever. What does this mean?

5. Verse 4 & 9 – Daniel is told warned that the full glory of that future cannot really be known until the end itself comes. Do we think too much or too little about that future? How should we think about it if it cannot yet be fully known?

6. Verses 5-7, 11 – Why does the One who 'lives forever' (verse 7) say that these 'astonishing things' will not come for 'three and half years'?

7. Verse 13 – After such a challenging and almost traumatic book, what is so great about the final verse?

Daniel

Study 6 Further Questions

1. There have been some Christian novels that imagine the spiritual conflicts going on in the spiritual realms. The Christians pray and this gives power to the angels who attack the demons. Is this sort of fiction helpful? Is it accurate to the Bible?

2. Down the centuries Christians have often thought that events prophesied in the Bible were happening right around them. In the 17th century Thomas Goodwin made a very convincing case that the world was about to end… only it didn't! In our day people tend to see prophecies fulfiled in the existence of the United Nations or the European Union or various middle eastern countries or different systems of making transactions or… any number of other features of modern life. Is this kind of speculation helpful? Does it create more or less focus on putting the teaching of Jesus into practice?

3. I remember hearing of a Christian woman who went into a strip club, climbed onto the stage and pointed at all the men present, declaring "you will all be judged for this. I will be there at the day of judgement to make sure that you are"! Do we need to recapture the reality and certainty of judgement day?

Study 6 Daily Readings

Day 1	Daniel 11:2-20
Day 2	Daniel 11:21-45
Day 3	Ezekiel 28:1-26
Day 4	Isaiah 14:3-15
Day 5	Daniel 12:1-13
Day 6	2 Peter 3:1-14
Day 7	Revelation 20:11-21:14

The daily Bible readings are an opportunity to not only read through all of the material in the book under study, but also to read parts of the Bible that relate to the themes and issues that we have been considering. We try to make sure that we receive light from the whole Bible as we think through the key issues each week.

Out of the frying pan

Suggested Answers to the Bible Study Questions

Study 1   Bible Answers

Daniel 2:14-23

1. Verse 14-15 – How was Daniel able to remain so calm when faced with sudden execution?

Daniel had already faced the loss of everything when he was abducted into Babylonian slavery. Instead of falling into despair or simply losing his identity and becoming 'Babylonian', Daniel slowly began to get a grip on his identity as a servant of the Living God. Daniel had entrusted himself to the LORD God and whether he lived or died he was at peace. Furthermore, he was filled with charismatic gifts (1:17) that helped him speak to Arioch with tact and wisdom.

2. Verse 16 – How could this foreign slave boy dare to negotiate with the great king Nebuchadnezzar? Can we think of examples like this in our own lives where we need great courage, wisdom and tact as we serve the Living God?

When we began to follow Jesus we took up our cross and followed Him: we counted ourselves as already dead as we took His life. If we have really understood this then we should no longer have any fear of mere human beings or any fear of death. Though Daniel was just a young teenager, far from home, far from the full church support he had always known, yet his feet were planted firmly on the Rock of Ages. Though young in years he was old in wisdom and maturity.

3. Verse 17 – What was Daniel's first course of action in this crisis?

Daniel may have lost the support of temple worship, the sacrifices and the teaching of the priests, nevertheless he had a small 'fellowship group' right there in Nebuchadnezzar's palace. He knew that he could not handle this alone. He needed the support of his church family, even if they were just as young and inexperienced as him. If we try to stand alone then we are doomed to fall.

4. Verse 18 – What was the second course of action? Shouldn't he have spent his time doing some 'dream research'?

Daniel

Having gathered his little 'home group' together, they set themselves to serious prayer. Their lives were on the line and the only hope they had was the miraculous intervention of the Living God. On earth they had no hope, but they had access to the 'God of heaven'. Notice that they pleaded for mercy. They knew that they had no right to be saved. They could not deserve the help of the LORD God – but they knew Him to be full of mercy and grace. Notice how specific their prayer was: they needed to know the content of the dream so that their lives could be saved. This was not a time for vague and general requests!

5. Verse 19 – The prayer was amazingly answered that very night while they were praying together. Can we recall any occasions when this has happened to us? Can we think of other occasions in the Bible when this has happened?

A good Biblical example is in Acts 12:1-19. The local church gathered together to pray for Peter's release, but when he was suddenly, marvellously released, they didn't want him to interrupt their prayer meeting!

6. Verses 19-20 – What was Daniel's immediate reaction to the answered prayer?

Daniel immediately wanted to praise the God if heaven. When our prayers are answered it is good to turn all our joy and relief and amazement directly to praise and worship. It can be easy to become so thrilled with the gift that we forget to thank the Giver.

7. Verse 20 – What qualities of the LORD God does Daniel first praise?

The very first quality is the wisdom of the LORD God. Throughout the chapter the very wisest of all the Babylonian experts acknowledged that Nebuchadnezzar's challenge was beyond them. Only the 'gods' could know these things… and yet they don't live among human beings – verse 11. Daniel is full of praise that the LORD God now only has the wisdom to know these deep mysteries but also the power to deliver them to an unworthy teenager like him.

8. Verse 21 – What does Daniel mean by the two parts of his prayer in this verse? Why doesn't the LORD God give wisdom to the foolish?

First Daniel acknowledges that although the human kings and rulers imagine that they hold all the power to steer history as they will, yet the real power lies with the God of heaven. The Living God decides what is going to happen and who is going to have any power.

Second, in the Bible the wise are those who fear the LORD and come to Him with humility and trust. The foolish are those who imagine that they are capable of handling life with their own resources. So, the LORD God gives His wisdom and knowledge to those who know that they have none of their own – those who cry out 'God be merciful to me, the sinner'.

9. Verses 22-23 – Even the very deepest and darkest secrets are obvious to the King of heaven. What impact would this night have had on the life of Daniel?

Daniel learned the reality of the LORD God in the fires of crisis. He may have known that these things were true from his study of the Scriptures when he was young, but now he had experienced the wisdom and mercy of the Living God in that desperate night of prayer. Have we ever experienced something like that? Have we forgotten what it meant to us or has it really shaped our lives?

Daniel

Study 2 Bible Answers

Daniel 3:13-30

1. Verses 13-14 – What is so strange about the words of Nebuchadnezzar? Think of the argument in Isaiah 40:9-20.

How strange it must have seemed to these three young men who had witnessed the incredible reality of the LORD God in that night of prayer with Daniel (2:17-19) when they were expected to treat a man-made statue as if it were a god! Nebuchadnezzar himself admits that he had made this 'god', yet he expects his 'wise men' to 'serve' it. If it were not so frightening it would be laughable.

2. What are the man-made things and ideas that we also serve? What are the golden idols that command our attention?

In Colossians 3:5 the apostle Paul reminds us that all greed is idolatry. Just because we don't form our gold into a human or animal shape doesn't mean that we don't worship it. If we get our security for the future and 'peace of mind' for the present from the 'golden' bank balances or pension schemes or investments, then we are the same as Nebuchadnezzar: we serve what our hands have made. What do we turn to when we are tired at the end of the day? What do we think gives us refreshment? What do we feel is 'missing' from our lives? Who or what do we wait on to renew our strength? (Compare Isaiah 40:28-31).

3. Verse 15 – Is it fair to say that Nebuchadnezzar was an atheist? Does he believe in any god other than his man-made statue?

Many people would claim to have some kind of a 'belief in god' or have some commitment to some kind of religion. Nevertheless our lives reveal what we really believe, what is real to us. Nebuchadnezzar assumes that there is no Living God who can actually do real things in the real world. What do we really believe? Do we live as if the LORD God really acts and responds to prayer, or do we basically go day after day in our own strength? Are we also 'practical atheists'?

4. Verses 16-18 – What do Shadrach, Meshach and Abednego believe in order to speak like this? How can they be so fearless when facing such a terrible fate?

These young men have already faced death. They have already let go of all the things they once held dear. They found that the LORD God is real and active and powerful. They know that He could easily save them from any circumstance if He chose to do so. However, they also know that His kingdom goes far beyond the limits of this mortal life. Whether we live or die doesn't matter at all: if we are absent from the body then we are present with Christ, which is far better (2 Corinthians 5:8). The glory of the Living God means more to us than our own safety or comfort. If we must die or lose everything in order to be faithful to Jesus, then we will accept that and trust Him to sustain us through the trial.

5. Verses 19-23 – Why was Nebuchadnezzar so enraged by the words of the young saints?

However angry Nebuchadnezzar was about their refusal to worship his man-made 'god' at least he assumed that these men would tremble in fear at his power and threats. When they clearly had no respect for this golden statue and had no fear of the consequences, then the weakness of all human power was revealed. As Jesus said, when we follow Him we do not need to have any fear of those who can only kill the body and then do no more (Matthew 10:28). Rather, when we fear the Real God then we need fear nothing else. Nebuchadnezzar hated the fact that these saints had unmasked the limited nature of his power, showing no fear before his ultimate threat. He must have felt so powerless when these saints witnessed to a Divine Kingdom that was so much more than ancient Babylon.

6. Verses 24-25 – Does it make any difference whether the fourth figure is just a created angel or the Son of God Himself, Jesus the LORD?

We all know what it is like when a boss gets an underling to do all his dirty work. If a boss sends his assistant to sack people or face the fire of criticism then we know that there is a deep character flaw. However, if the boss spends personal time with the employees, even in the hardest times, then he gets such respect.

In the same way, it matters a great deal whether the LORD God of heaven is prepared to come to His saints when they are in this most terrible trial.

It would be good if he sent some support from a created angel, but what amazing grace and glory that He came Himself! The fact that the Living God is closest to us in the hardest times is His glory.

7. Verse 26 – What has changed about Nebuchadnezzar?

He did not believe that any god could save from his fierce furnace (verse 15), but now he recognises that these three men are nothing less than servants of the Most High God. Notice how he personally comes to call them out rather than sending a servant, as if he forgot all about chains of command in his amazement.

8. Verses 27 – Why is it important to see that the fire had not harmed them in any way? Why bother noting that there was not even the smell of smoke?

Human beings might be able to design clothes that resist the heat, but not clothes that bear no sign of the fire or heat. This was far beyond any human explanation. Furthermore, many of us worry that we will never be able to recover from the fires of suffering and tragedy that we have to go through. On that resurrection morning, I wonder if we will find that not even the smell of the smoke will be left on us.

9. Verses 28-30 – What are the most remarkable features of Nebuchadnezzar's praise?

First, Nebuchadnezzar did not believe in the reality of the LORD God an hour before and now he was shouting His praises as if he had always believed it!

Second, notice how he recognises the fact that the Most High God sent His Angel to rescue His servants.

Third, Nebuchadnezzar praises the LORD God that these men defied him and trusted in Him instead. Before he was furious but now full of wonder that they were willing to die for the Living God.

Four, he no longer believes in any other God!

Study 3   Bible Answers

Daniel 6:1-10

1. Verses 1-2 – How could Daniel work in such a senior position for a godless, pagan nation? How can a believer work for such an ungodly system?

Daniel had faced this question long before when he was first abducted into the Babylonian empire. He had to deal with his true citizenship at that time. Think of Paul's teaching in Philippians 3:18-21 - "Their destiny is destruction, their god is their stomach, and their glory is in their shame. Their mind is on earthly things. *But our citizenship is in heaven.* And we eagerly await a Saviour from there, the Lord Jesus Christ, who, by the power that enables him to bring everything under his control, will transform our lowly bodies so that they will be like his glorious body." We are always involved in systems that are not the kingdom of the Living God. Even if we work in a church environment, so much of what happens falls far short of the divine glory. No, we do not get our identity from where we work, but from the one we ultimately work for – no matter what career we pursue.

2. Verse 3 – How did Daniel come to have such exceptional abilities? (Remember chapter 1:15-20).

The LORD God did not abandon Daniel to face the challenges of his career alone in the Babylonian civil service. Daniel showed that he wanted to honour the LORD in all he did, so the LORD blessed him in his work. Daniel was determined to bring glory to God through his faithful witness and integrity, so he was given all the wisdom he needed for that challenging world – see also James 1:5.

3. Verses 3-4 – Why is it so important for our work to be of the highest level we can possibly achieve? If the 'praise of men' is of no final value, why should we work so hard to show integrity and excellence in our work?

It is not our own glory that is at stake. If we are known to be those who bear the Name of the LORD Jesus, then the way we live, the way we speak, and the way we work are all statements about the character and glory of

Daniel

Jesus. If His own people cannot be trusted, fiddling expenses, grabbing for money or prestige, then we drag the Name of Jesus into our own filth and shame. The way we live is the loudest sermon we ever preach. The words we speak about Jesus will be drowned out by our shoddy work.

4. Verse 5 – Daniel could not be attacked professionally, so he had to be attacked in terms of his commitment to the LORD God. How might this happen today? How do people try to upset or provoke us concerning our love for Jesus?

The very fact that we witness through our lives and words means that there will always be those around us who react badly to that. They may feel condemned as we shine like lights in the darkness or they may feel we are arrogant or weak or judgemental. Sometimes people use foul language and religious swearing in order to attack us. Maybe they try to tempt us into bad behaviour or compromised situations.

1 Peter 2:12-15 - "Live such good lives among the pagans that, though they accuse you of doing wrong, they may see your good deeds and glorify God on the day he visits us. Submit yourselves for the Lord's sake to every authority instituted among men... For it is God's will that by doing good you should silence the ignorant talk of foolish men."

5. Verses 6-9 – What does this speech tell us about the enemies of Daniel? Is their speech honest or deceitful?

First of all they try to flatter the king. Then they give the impression that there was a unanimous verdict about this decree – verse 7 – even though Daniel, the most senior and respected of all the administrators, knew nothing about it. They make the king feel as if he were as important as a god, which is always poison in anyone's ear. They also made sure that the king committed to this course of action in writing before he could change his mind. They knew that he would think better of this after a night's sleep. If Daniel was honoured by the way he lived, these men were shamed by their own lives and behaviour.

6. Verse 10 – Why did Daniel continue to pray three times a day even when he knew about the decree?

Daniel was well known for his life and practice. He was known as a man of prayer. If he were to stop praying or only pray secretly then he would

give the impression that the fear of humans weighed more heavily than the fear of the Living God. However, Daniel did not say his prayers out in the public square or march into the office praying 6 times a day in a loud voice. Daniel simply carried on as he had always done. He didn't seek out confrontation, but neither did he run from it.

7. When is it right to come into conflict with the law and when is it right to avoid the conflict? In a democracy do we also have the added responsibility of speaking out about the laws that might create such conflicts?

We need great wisdom in this. We should disobey the state only as a last resort. We are commanded to show respect and obedience to every authority, so it may well be disobedience against God if we too readily decide to defy the law. Yet, there may be times when it is impossible to obey both God and humanity.

In the same way, we need great wisdom in speaking out about laws. The great danger is that we become narrowly focussed on only one set of concerns, from one political perspective – whether simply looking at issues of sexually morality or only issues of international relief or environmental care. This is why we need the accountability and balance of a local church family, so that we listen to those who see what we do not see and have courage and wisdom that we might not have.

Daniel

Study 4   Bible Answers

Daniel 7:9-18

1. Verse 9 – Why is there more than one throne in heaven? How can there be other thrones alongside the throne of the Ancient of Days?

Jesus seems to share the one throne with His Father. In verses 13-14 we will see the Son of Man who is able to approach the Ancient of Days as an equal. The Ancient of Days is God the Father and the Son of Man is Jesus Christ. Jesus sits at the right hand of the Father on high – but according to Revelation 4:2 and 22:3 they have the same throne.

However, the utterly incredible truth is that we are invited to share in their reign over the whole creation. Note how in verse 18 how the 'saints of the Most High' also inherit the kingdom. As the followers of Jesus, as His Bride and Body, we reign with Him. If He is the Eternal Son of the Father, then we are joined to Him as adopted brothers and sisters.

2. Verse 9 – The description of the Ancient of Days is amazing and glorious. How does it compare to the description of Jesus in Revelation 1:12-16? Can we see a family resemblance?

There are obviously related! We might sometimes comment how a son looks just like his father, but we really must say this of the Eternal Father and Son!

3. Verse 9 – In the description of Jesus in Revelation 1, we learn something about His face. Why doesn't Daniel see the face of the Ancient of Days? Why doesn't anybody ever tell us what His face looks like?

Nobody has ever seen the Father's face at any time. When Moses asked if he could see the LORD who remained hidden in the thick darkness, (Exodus 33:19-23) the LORD said, "you cannot see my face, for no one may see me and live." Then the LORD said, "There is a place near me where you may stand on a rock. When my glory passes by, I will put you in a cleft in the rock and cover you with my hand until I have passed by. Then I will remove my hand and you will see my back; but my face must not be seen." See also John 1:18.

4. Verse 10 – Why is heaven like a court? What are the books that were opened?

Surrounded by more than 100 million angels (10,000 times 10,000), all ready to instantly carry out any command, the scene is awe-inspiring. Yet, there is serious business to do. On the one hand we can think how earthly kings used to hold court and allow people to come before them with their requests. However, it is more likely that we are to think here of a trial where evidence is presented and a judgement given. The books contain a record of all that has happened on the earth, the details of every life. Revelation 20:11-12 - "I saw a great white throne and him who was seated on it. Earth and sky fled from his presence, and there was no place for them. 12 And I saw the dead, great and small, standing before the throne, and books were opened. Another book was opened, which is the book of life. The dead were judged according to what they had done as recorded in the books."

5. Verse 11-12 – How can these disturbing verses actually be a great comfort to us in this present age? Who would most appreciate these verses?

If we read on in Revelation 21:13-15 we see how on that final day of Justice, everything will be properly examined and judged. Nothing can be hidden under the carpet any longer. All the dark secrets and terrible hidden crimes will finally be dealt with and all the countless victims will be given justice.

So many powerless people have suffered under evil regimes and nothing has ever been done about it. It seems that nobody even knows about it. Yet, it is all recorded in the courts of heaven. For so many people the only possible hope and comfort is that justice belongs to the Living God and He will repay – Deut 32:35; Romans 12:19.

6. Verse 13-14 – On the basis of these verses, how would we describe the Son of Man?

Surrounded by heavenly glory, He has been given everything that the Ancient of Days possesses. He has been appointed to rule the Kingdom of Heaven. All humanity, in every nation, speaking every language, in every age of the world must bow before Him – whether willingly or

Daniel

unwillingly. His kingdom will never be replaced by a greater one, because the Son of Man and His kingdom is the greatest and highest and final reality.

7. Verses 13 – What are the 'clouds of heaven'?

Jesus mentions these clouds in His own teaching – Matt 26:64; Mark 14:62. Perhaps at the very least it means that He will be coming down from the sky on that final day – that just as He ascended above the clouds, so He will return in the same way. It seems that heaven is full of such bright and shining glory that it might look something like brilliant, beautiful clouds. When He designed our world, Jesus put clouds into the sky to help us get a sense of the vast glory and light that surrounds Him. It is well worth spending time gazing on and meditating on the clouds in the sky. They can be dark and angry in the storm, yet they also give us the essential water that gives us life. They especially draw our attention to the sunrise and the sunset – both key moments of each day.

8. Verse 18 – If someone asked us how we might become one of these saints who inherits this everlasting kingdom, what would we say?

It might be good to begin with the fact of the books that record everything about us to be used in evidence on that final Day of Justice. What do these books contain about each one of us? We can never inherit the Heavenly Kingdom so long as these offences remain on record. The Son of Man is not only the King but also the Saviour. He came down from heaven to make it possible for anybody and everybody to enter the kingdom with a clean sheet. Jesus Himself said "the Son of Man did not come to be served, but to serve, and to give his life as a ransom for many" (Mark 10:45). He came to die (Mark 8:31) and rise again to make a way to get to the other side of Judgement Day – as if the Day of opening books and judgement were already past.

This is why there are people in every culture and language who worship Him with such great joy and gratitude.

Study 5 Bible Answers

Daniel 9:4-19

1. Verse 4 – Why does Daniel begin with such a high view of the LORD God? If he feels so bad about his sin, doesn't that simply make it all seem worse?

Remember the Lord's prayer, taught by Jesus. We must begin with a high view of our Father in heaven or else the problem of our sin will seem beyond hope. If our sin is such a big problem, then we need to remember that the One we are speaking to is even greater. Only our Saviour God is able to do the impossible: make us welcome in his holy kingdom.

2. Verse 4 – The covenant is the plan of salvation, the gospel set out by the Trinity from before the world began. How does Daniel describe the covenant?

He calls it the covenant 'of love'. Some might think it is a covenant of obedience, but it is impossible to please God with works – Hebrews 11:6. When Jesus was asked what it is all about, what God really wants from us, He replied that we are love Him with everything in us. He loves us more than we can ever know and He has gone to infinite lengths to show this love to us, even dying a God-forsaken death for us. If we love Him and follow Him, then in spite of all our sin, He will save us.

3. Verses 5-6 – List all the verbs that are used to describe the way we have betrayed our loving LORD. Which ones speak to us most?

Sinned; done wrong; been wicked; rebelled; turned away; not listened.

4. Verses 7-11 – Why does Daniel list all the sins of earlier generations? Why take responsibility for things he didn't even do?

Daniel knew his own heart. As he read the Scripture record of the sins of his forefathers, he knew that the same unfaithfulness and hard-heartedness was in him too. When we read of the grumbling on the Exodus, or the unbelief of Israel, or the way the disciples want to avoid the Cross, we must recognise that same wicked, unbelieving heart in ourselves. Think of Adam & Eve. Until we can acknowledge that we betray the LORD in the same way, time and time again, then we will never know the full-hearted repentance that we need.

Daniel

5. Verses 11b-14 – In the Law, why did the LORD God describe the consequences of rejecting His law in such detail? Why spend more time on the curses rather than the blessings? See Deuteronomy 28:15-68.

When the LORD set the Law before His people He knew that the sinful human heart loves the darkness and is always tempted to sink into unbelief and selfishness. Jeremiah 17:9 - "The heart is deceitful above all things and beyond cure. Who can understand it? I the LORD search the heart and examine the mind…" The reason that Jesus warns of Hell more than anyone else in the Bible is because He loves us so deeply. With our own children, when we know how careless they are we impress on them the dangers with all the passion we can muster. In spite of the lengthy warnings and the incredible patience of the LORD God of Israel, even still the curses of the Law did fall on the ancient church. These things were written for our example – 1 Corinthians 10:1-6. In this generation the church may suffer the same judgement from her Lord – consider Revelation 2:4-5.

6. Verses 15-19 – What is the basis of Daniel's prayer for mercy?

He cannot ask for mercy on the basis of any good things that he or any other sinful humans have done. If we have betrayed the love of our LORD so often and so deeply, then there is nothing in us that can improve the situation. Rather Daniel appeals to the Name and nature of the Living God Himself. He remembers the great acts of salvation in the past and the glory that these brought to the Name of the Lord. He remembers that the Lord is righteous. The righteousness of the Lord does not only mean that He will punish the wicked but also that He will save those who call on Him – Psalm 4:1; 116:5; 145:17; Zechariah 9:9. Daniel even appeals to the fact that His church is laughed at in its weakness.

7. What lessons can we learn for our own prayer life? Spend some time now praying a Daniel 9 prayer of repentance. How can we repent for the weakness, the lack of practical love and the betrayal of living truth in recent generations?

Study 6   Bible Answers

Daniel 12:1-13

1. Verse 1 – Don't spend too long on this question, but do we feel convinced that Michael is Christ? What are the arguments for and against?

The name Michael means 'One like God'. Throughout Daniel he is referred to as the great Prince who cares for the church. Notice that He is not associated with any of the human nations. In this verse, 12:1, we learn that when Michael arises then all the church is delivered from its greatest peril. In Revelation 12:7 Michael is the Commander of the angelic army (the LORD of hosts) and he defeats the rebellion of Satan. The more difficult verse might be Jude 9. If Jude is the physical brother of Jesus, why refer to Him in such a strange way? On the other hand, the incident he refers to is almost certainly Zechariah 3:1-2 where it is the Angel of the LORD who speaks to Satan, who is clearly the LORD Jesus.

2. Verse 1 – Throughout the book of Daniel the church is warned that terrible persecution lies ahead. Jesus tells His followers the same thing – Luke 21:12; John 15:20. Paul repeats this teaching in general – 2 Timothy 3:12 – and in particular concerning a time of unprecedented persecution – 2 Thessalonians 2:1-12. The book of Revelation also seems to indicate severe persecution before Jesus returns. Why do we need to know this?

The world, the flesh and the devil always want to destroy the church. The easiest way of doing this is to make us into the world, to make us feel so comfortable and at home in this passing darkness that we forget the coming age of light and glory. We can so easily feel that the world loves us, or loves us as long as we keep quiet. However, no matter how lovingly we behave, we will still be persecuted, just like Jesus. He lived with more love and understanding and patience than anyone, yet the religious and political powers still had to persecute and kill Him. We must expect the same. If the world is in rebellion against the Kingdom of Heaven, then as agents of that kingdom we must be ready for opposition – not so that we become defensive or aggressive, but so that we are not surprised or demoralised when the suffering and opposition comes.

3. Verses 1-2 – From dust we came and to dust we return… until that final day of resurrection. Why is *everybody* resurrected, whether good or evil – whether for life or for shame?

That day of resurrection is also the day of justice. The church will have lived through such terrible times of darkness and injustice. Terrible evil will have been committed, things that now we hear only whispers of. That day will be the day when the lights are switched on and everything will be laid bare. All who have ever live must be brought back to answer for the way they lived, for the crimes they committed, whether in thought, word or action. For those who chose the hard way of life, following Jesus on the narrow way that leads to life, that day will be the day of finally entering into rest and comfort. For those who went along the broad way of comfort and rest in this passing age, on that final day the God of Justice will show contempt for such lives of unbelief, selfishness and cowardice.

4. Verse 3 – The followers of Jesus will be like the bright heavens and the stars forever and ever. What does this mean?

The "bright heavens" means the bright sky. For most of us around the world (drought sufferers excepted), there is something wonderful about gazing up at a bright sky with the sun shining. The sky is blue, the clouds of heaven drift across the serene expanse in their towering glory. The angel-like winged creatures of the heavens go about their business in that free and open realm. Light and life pour down from those bright heavens lifting every plant, animal and human who will respond to its daily act of worship. In that new creation future, there will be no night. The Father and the Son will fill the whole creation with endless light and life, like the brightest and best day that never ends.

Then in that second heaven, the expanse that we tend to call 'space', there are so many majestic 'suns' burning with a glorious splendour, roaming through that even larger arena of freedom and wonder. What it will be like to be given the freedom of that realm, rather than cooped into ludicrous 'spaceships' of science fiction!

5. Verse 4 & 9- Daniel is told warned that the full glory of that future cannot really be known until the end itself comes. Do we think too much or too little about that future? How should we think about it if it cannot yet be fully known?

Most people seem to take the warning of verse 4 & 9 too far. All too often we don't bother thinking about our resurrection hope because it seems to be unimaginable. Yet, many of us do have certain fixed ideas about it, not all of which are helpful. Many of us imagine, for example, that the future is a ghost-like state in an ethereal realm or even that it is like an infinitely long church service. However, the Bible gives us many descriptions and explanations of the kind of physical life that we can look forward to – planting vineyards, eating feasts, living in houses and interacting with the animals. After His resurrection, Jesus showed us what that future would look like – walking, eating, and enjoying time with His friends. The full picture remains hidden, beyond our wildest dreams, and yet enough glimpses of the picture are given to us to allow us to fill our hearts and minds with great hope and joy.

6. Verses 5-7, 11 – Why does the One who 'lives forever' (verse 7) say that these 'astonishing things' will not come for 'three and half years'?

The history of the church has been a lot longer than 'three and a half years' since Daniel wrote – and yet we have the same concerns and fears for the church that Daniel knew. The persecution goes on. Around the world today there are Christians facing situations like Antiochus Epiphanes and Vespasian. At different times there have been terrible massacres of the church in different areas of the world. This will happen in the future – perhaps to us. Yet, from the perspective of 'the One who lives forever' this long period of conflict and persecution is such a short time. It is almost as if He were saying, "in half the time in took to make the world, it will all be over!" Yes, the our power may be broken through this time, yet we need to constantly remind ourselves that none of this will last forever. The end is not far away. The Judge is standing at the very door. The night is far spent and the dawn is at hand.

7. Verse 13 – After such a challenging and almost traumatic book, what is so great about the final verse?

We may well become so concerned about all that we have read in Daniel. We might feel anxious about the prophesied persecutions. We might feel that we can identify the next world figure who might bring such a time on the church. We might get all worked up about 'reading the times' and trying to defend against this fore-ordained opposition. However, these reactions are not the right and wise reaction. The book of Daniel has taught us, above all else, that the whole of history is in the hands of the LORD Jesus. He cares for His church far better than we ever can. Our job is to follow His Way, obey His truth and live His life with all the love and peace and joy that are in the Holy Spirit. Then we will die and rest with Him until that glorious day of resurrection. That is out true future – and whatever momentary trouble we pass through on the way should never disturb that deep peace that He gives to us.